WISDOM
AND HUMANNESS
IN PSYCHOLOGY

Wisdom and Humanness in Psychology

Prospects for a Christian Approach

C. Stephen Evans

REGENT COLLEGE PUBLISHING
VANCOUVER, BRITISH COLUMBIA

Original edition published 1989
by Baker Book House,
Grand Rapids MI 49516   (ISBN 0-8010-3449-3)

This edition published by Regent College Publishing.

This volume is based on lectures given at the Finch Symposium at Fuller
Graduate School of Psychology, January 1988.

Regent College Publishing is an imprint of Regent College Bookstore,
5800 University Boulevard, Vancouver, B.C. V6T 2E4 Canada

Printed in Canada

First printing   1996
Second printing   1997

Library of Congress Cataloguing in Publication Data

Evans, C. Stephen.
  Wisdom and humanness in psychology / C. Stephen Evans.

     161 p.   22 cm.
  Bibliography: p.
  Includes index.
  1. Psychology and religion. 2. Christianity—Psychology.
3. Psychology–Philosophy.   I. Title.

BF51.E915   1997

ISBN 1-57383-065-8

To
Arthur Holmes
From whom I caught the vision
for integrating faith and learning

Contents

Preface   9

1. Can Psychology Be Christian?   11
    The Dominant Paradigm in Psychology:
    Empiricism and Its Problems
    Why *Not* Christian Psychology?

2. The Three Faces of Psychology   23
    The Empirical Face of Psychology
    The Interpretive Face of Psychology
    The Critical Face of Psychology
    The Interdependence of the Three Faces

3. The Hermeneutical Dimension of Empirical
    Psychology   45
    Human Activity as Constituted by Meaning
    Observing Meaningful Behavior
    The Place of Meaning in Empirical Studies

4. Taking Meaning Seriously in Psychology   67
    Introspection and Recollection
    Psychology and Wisdom
    The Contributions of Other Human Sciences
    The Contributions of Literature

The Contributions of Philosophy
The Contribution of Christian Learning
Reflections on Meaning: *Two Case Studies*

5. Taking Values Seriously in Psychology   87
   The Divorce of Facts and Values
   What Is Value-Free Science?
   Should All Concepts in Psychology Be Value-Free?
   Do Facts Alone Determine Which Theories Should Be Held?
   Reasons and Rationalizations: *Evaluating the Other's Story*

6. Taking Freedom Seriously in Psychology   109
   The Significance of Freedom for Christian Psychology
   The Nature of Determinism: *Hard and Soft*
   The Nature of Freedom
   Scientific Objections to Libertarianism
   Hermeneutics and Freedom
   Christian Psychology and Basic Assumptions

7. Christian Psychology: *The Impossible Dream?*   131
   The Nature of Christian Psychology
   Christian Psychology: *Science or Ideology?*
   Hermeneutics and the Limits of Technique
   A Future and a Hope

Suggestions for Additional Reading   145

Index   157

Preface

This book had its genesis in the invitation I received from the Graduate School of Psychology of Fuller Theological Seminary to deliver the featured lectures at the Finch Symposium in January of 1988. I am deeply grateful to Fuller for providing me the occasion and stimulus to rethink some of the issues in the philosophy of psychology that I first tackled more than ten years ago in *Preserving the Person*. Readers of that first book will, I hope, see development and growth in my ideas, but also continuity.

I had originally planned to deliver the Finch lectures on the theme of "Kierkegaard as a Model for Christian Psychology," a project on which I am still at work and hope to bring to fruition soon. However, as I began to think about this theme, it became clear to me that some preliminary spade work was necessary. The conception of psychology which dominates American academic psychology today is such that it is difficult for psychologists, even Christian psychologists, to see Kierkegaard as a psychologist in the contemporary sense. Before he can serve as a model for Christian psychology, our conception of psychology must be transformed. This book is an attempt to encourage such a transformation. It is offered in the hope that such a change is a realistic possibility, because the new vision which is offered has enough continuity with present conceptions for the change to be seen as a fulfillment and a deepening, rather than a rejection, of the fine work that currently goes on in psychology.

Besides thanking Fuller for the invitation, I would like to express my gratitude for the friendly reception the lectures received, and the helpful discussion which followed. I also want to express my deep appreciation to Stanton Jones of Wheaton College and to my colleagues Alan Tjeltveit and Fred Stoutland of St. Olaf College for reading the manuscript and making numerous helpful suggestions. Finally, I am very much in the debt of Hendrika Vande Kemp for supplying the helpful list of suggested readings at the end of the book.

Can Psychology Be Christian?

With a somewhat whimsical use of medieval categories, Alvin Plantinga has classified Christians trying to integrate Christianity with the sciences into three groups: Averroists, Thomists, and Augustinians.[1] Averroists are named after the Arabic philosopher Averroes, who taught a doctrine of twofold truth which allowed that a proposition could be true in theology but false in a science and vice versa. Modern-day Averroists either compartmentalize their faith from their work as scholars and therefore do not notice any tensions, or else they cheerfully embrace some version of Averroes's own doctrine of twofold truth. I believe the number of Christians who actually fall into this group is small and getting smaller all the time in the midst of a heightened concern with integrating faith and learning.

Thomists, obviously named after the great Catholic philosopher of the thirteenth century, Thomas Aquinas, al-

1. Taken from an unpublished talk given at a conference on "A New Agenda for Evangelical Thought," sponsored by I.F.A.C.S. at Wheaton College, June 3-6, 1987.

low for a variety of positive relationships between Christian faith and the scholarly life. To begin with, they deny what the Averroists affirm; truth in one field does not conflict with truth in another. So Thomists at least demand that Christian faith and the conclusions of scholarship be consistent.

Typically Thomists demand much more than this as well. Thomists usually look for mutual support between the conclusions of scholarship and the convictions of faith, since all truth is viewed as coming from God. There are other helpful ways in which faith and learning might be of help to each other. One might argue that the personal qualities which genuine Christian faith engenders in people, such as honesty and kindness, are especially conducive to making people productive members of scientific communities. From the other side, the knowledge gained through inquiry may be useful and even essential for Christians who want to express their religious and moral convictions in practical, effective ways.

Despite these positive relations, and others which could be mentioned, the Thomistic view still sees the relations between faith and learning as primarily external in nature. However harmonious and cooperative faith and science may be, they are still autonomous enterprises, and this is seen by the Thomist as a virtue, not a fault. So the Christian who is a scientist inevitably wears at least two hats, and she must be clear about which hat she is wearing at which time.

The Augustinian view accepts the positive, external relationships which the Thomist accepts, but insists that there are also positive, internal ways that faith can be related to learning. The Christian who is a biologist should not only be a good biologist; she ought at least to consider the possibility of approaching biology from a distinctively Christian perspective.

The Dominant Paradigm in Psychology:
Empiricism and Its Problems

It is clear that the majority of Christian psychologists are at present Thomists in their view of how Christianity should relate to psychology. They are happy when psychology supports views which they see as consistent with Christianity, and happy to point out parallels between biblical teachings and psychological insights. They are concerned to bring Christian perspectives to bear on ethical issues that confront psychologists, and hopeful that psychological knowledge will be helpful to the church when applied in various areas. However, the notion of a distinctively Christian psychology has found few supporters, and those supporters have found much resistance and opposition among their psychologist colleagues.

This is because psychologists by and large still accept a certain view of their discipline as a science. If psychology is to be a science, they believe, it must be characterized by a commitment to the scientific method, which is thought to be an objective, neutral route to truth. Without trying to be too precise, it is fair to say that the view of the scientific method which underlies psychology is strongly empiricist. In this view of science, what distinguishes genuine science from pseudoscience or nonscience is a willingness to test theories empirically. Theories are tested by observable facts, and facts are supposed to be relatively theory-free, as they must be if they are going to provide the test which theories have to pass.

Psychologists have of course long since gone beyond simple, naive versions of empiricism. Thus, most psychologists today would reject inductivism, the view that theories are developed and confirmed by repeated observations. Theories are developed in a host of ways that involve intuition and imagination, and theories are scientific not if they can be empirically proven, an impossible task, but if they are treated as vulnerable to empirical falsification.

Even with these modifications, however, the empiricist view of science leads only to a Thomistic view of the integration of religion and science, never an Augustinian one. Christian convictions might function in helping the researcher select a topic to study, since some issues might seem especially important to a Christian. Christian convictions might lead the scientist to propose some hypotheses rather than others, and this is legitimate, since liberal empiricism allows for personal intuitions and hunches to play a role in the "context of discovery." However, in the all-important (for science) context of justification, Christian convictions must be put aside; here objectivity reigns. Here one's Christian faith can only play a role in buttressing the scientist's commitment to be the best scientist he or she can be. Distinctively Christian values do not reappear until knowledge is being applied.

The shortcomings of this empiricist philosophy of science are by now well-known and well-documented.[2] One does not have to go to the extreme relativism of Paul K. Feyerabend or even accept some of the relativistic excesses of Thomas Kuhn to disagree with empiricism. The problems are familiar, so I will attempt only a brief summary.

One grave problem is that the move to falsificationism, the claim that what makes a theory scientific is its susceptibility to falsification by facts, does not really solve the problem of showing how theories are supported by empirical facts. The falsificationists reason that it is impossible to conclusively show that empirical theories are true, since further data could always overturn the conclusions reached. For similar reasons probabilistic positive confirmation is problematic, since probability theory re-

2. For a judicious and balanced summary of these criticisms, see chapters 3 and 4 of Del Ratzsch, *Philosophy of Science: The Natural Sciences in Christian Perspective* (Downers Grove: Inter-Varsity, 1986).

quires a well-delimited domain of instances, and empirical data are open-ended. Merely one negative instance, however, is sufficient to falsify a universal law for the falsificationist, who therefore makes the success of a theory depend on its capacity to withstand falsification.

What falsificationists do not seem to notice is that falsificationism is vulnerable to comparable difficulties. When a well-confirmed theory is apparently disconfirmed by one counterinstance, the scientist does not necessarily have to view the theory as falsified. He may, and often does, choose to reject the data as spurious or flawed. Indeed, the practice of ignoring odd data in order to draw a smooth curve is common enough to have a name in psychology; it is termed "windsorizing" the data.

In any case, it is rare indeed when a theory can be isolated and made to face the data alone. The rule is to systematically connect theories in a web. When such a web of theories is apparently falsified, even when the scientist accepts the data as genuine, no particular theory need be thrown out. Any of a number of interconnected theories may be modified.

In addition, the falsificationist must come to terms with the fact that it is hardly ever the case that a single set of theories survives the test of falsifiability. Theories are usually underdetermined by data, and the choice between theories which are supported equally well by empirical data must be made on the basis of value criteria which are extra-empirical, such as simplicity, elegance, and fertility.

In addition to the problems of deriving theory solely from facts, the empiricist faces another serious nest of problems in the whole notion of "facts." To the extent that facts are not independent of theory, they cannot provide an independent confirmation of theory. Yet most philosophers of science are now agreed that facts are more or less heavily theory-laden, and "all seeing is seeing-as." Theory-free description of facts is impossible simply because every description must be made in language, and language is itself always theory-laden. There are no immaculate perceptions; even if there were, there would be no immaculate concepts to describe them.

These points are well-known, and some individuals have employed them to embrace a relativistic view which despairs of finding truth or genuine knowledge. Such desperation seems both unnecessary and unwise. Contemporary philosophers of science have gradually developed a middle-of-the-road position which takes note of the role played by values and subjectivity in science as a historical endeavor without concluding that seeing those factors overwhelms any chance of gaining genuine knowledge.[3]

But even a moderate philosophy of science which wishes to avoid relativism must today accept that philosophical assumptions and personal values often play a positive role in science. If this is so, then it would appear that Christian psychologists would at least be open to the possibility of a distinctively Christian psychology, a psychology which would reflect distinctively Christian convictions and values, just as feminist and Marxist psychology reflect feminist and Marxist convictions and values.

Why *Not* Christian Psychology?

In reality, most Christian psychologists have been reluctant to propose such a thing. Why? The most obvious answer is that psychologists are still committed to empiricism; they have not yet been persuaded by the powerful philosophical critique of this position. This answer is correct as far as it goes, but in one sense it is no answer at all. We still do not know *why* psychologists cling so tenaciously to empiricism.

3. See chapters 4 and 5 of Ratzsch, *Philosophy of Science,* and the endnotes to those chapters for additional reading in this area.

Actually, the entrenched resistance to changing the nature of psychology is precisely what one would expect if Kuhn's view of scientific change is correct.[4] According to Kuhn, a particular scientific community is wedded to what he terms a paradigm, and change does not come easily in such a case. The members of the scientific community absorb the paradigm in the process of being socialized into the community; their very identity as scientists is closely tied to the paradigm. This is largely true of psychologists, who are still taught that psychology came into being as a science in the late nineteenth and early twentieth centuries when its heroic forefathers put aside philosophical speculation and seriously began to look for facts in accordance with *the* scientific method. It is difficult for psychologists who have accepted this view of their field and themselves to consider other alternatives seriously.

Other factors as well have worked to block the development of Christian psychology. Chief among these are the crudeness and low quality of much of what is called "Christian" or "biblical" psychology. Christian psychologists are understandably reluctant to identify with a low-quality product which is unlikely to be taken seriously by their professional peers. (I do think Christian psychologists should in some cases risk the disapproval of their non-Christian peers. I will say more about this in the final chapter.)

Other factors which might be mentioned in addition to the low quality of much Christian psychology include the degree to which Christian academics have been affected by the privatizing of religion in the West.[5] People who are accustomed to thinking of religious commitment as "individual" and "personal," and who do not think of living

4. See Thomas Kuhn, *The Structure of Scientific Revolutions* (Chicago: University of Chicago Press, 1962).

5. See Robert Bellah and associates, *Habits of the Heart* (Berkeley: University of California Press, 1985), for an illuminating discussion of the effects of individualistic, "privatized" religion on culture.

faith as something which shapes the central institutions of a culture, naturally do not consider the potential of Christian faith to reshape an academic discipline. Many Christian academics do not make much of an effort to think in a Christian manner about their discipline. When we add to these factors the special professional milieu which surrounds psychologists today, the problems are accentuated, particularly among applied psychologists, who function in an atmosphere which places heavy emphasis on materialistic and pragmatic values. The American Psychological Association acts as a gatekeeper for the profession and is generally hostile to seeing psychology as tied in any intrinsic way to religion. Many applied psychologists also receive third-party payments which place them in a public context where religious commitments are seen as the kind of personal, private factor which must be excluded.

Whatever the reasons for the tenacity of the old paradigm, we must recognize that in Kuhn's view a paradigm is not displaced until a new, more attractive paradigm is available to supplant it. So if Kuhn is right, we cannot expect the empiricist paradigm to be replaced until powerful exemplars of research which conform to a different paradigm are present and publicized.

The primary need, therefore, is not for people to talk about the problems with the old paradigm or the desirability of a new one. It is, rather, for psychologists to demonstrate the power of a new approach by actual scientific work. One should not, however, underestimate the difficulty of doing this. In particular, it would be unrealistic and illogical to expect research done under the new paradigm to excel when judged by the criteria which are part and parcel of the old approach. For this reason Kuhn suggests that a new paradigm is finally victorious only when the partisans of the old approach die off and are unable to win enough converts among the younger generation. Insurgents, however, are at a great disadvantage in the present cultural situation, where science is so heavily dependent on research money controlled by the establishment.

Still, the situation is by no means impossible. The demise of radical behaviorism and the rise of cognitive approaches in psychology over the last fifteen to twenty years, though a change within the dominant paradigm, show that at least minirevolutions are possible.

Christian psychologists who are interested in exploring distinctively Christian approaches to the field face a classic chicken-and-egg problem. On the one hand, new exemplars of research and theory are unlikely to have much impact unless they are carried out by people who are highly respected in the field. This implies that the first task of Christian psychologists is to win credibility: play the game by the established rules, publish, go to the best graduate schools, get prestigious positions. The problem is that in doing those things, Christian psychologists are highly likely to be conditioned into a wholehearted acceptance of the dominant paradigm. If they try to avoid this by avoiding centers of power, they are unlikely to have much of an impact.

Practically, this difficulty can be overcome only by a two-front strategy. Young, talented Christian psychologists must be trained to be first-rate scholars who can and do play by the established rules. Simultaneously, these scholars must be taught, nurtured, and encouraged to keep their critical faculties intact and to creatively envision alternative ways of studying human beings. This task can be accomplished only if at least a few established Christian psychologists can be converted to new possibilities, and can therefore, with the help of Christian theologians and philosophers, encourage the new generation to think boldly.

Therefore, though the first priority is work, not talk, a certain amount of talk is still necessary. A minority of the gifted psychologists, primarily younger scholars but also some older scholars with established credibility, must experience a conversion powerful enough to motivate them to risk something for the sake of the idea of Christian psychology. A critical nucleus is necessary, because a new paradigm cannot be established without a critical mass of resources and a community of people who can support and provide helpful criticism for each other's work.

What I want to do in this book is not to beat the oft-beaten horse of empiricism again, but to write concretely, to the degree that it is possible for a nonpsychologist to do so, about the character of psychology conceived in a nonempiricist (though still empirical) mode. Such a psychology, committed to empirical research but free from the shackles of empiricism, would not differ as much from the dominant paradigm in psychology as some advocates of a humanized psychology believe. While to some this may lessen the urgency of the appeal, I believe that it enhances its credibility. It makes conversion of some current practitioners a real possibility, because it means that they could move toward a new conception of psychology which is still recognizable to them as psychology. They could open themselves to some alternative research strategies without repudiating current strategies or rejecting their own identity as psychologists who have successfully worked within the empiricist paradigm.

The new psychology I have in mind would obviously be one which is congenial to distinctively Christian insights. Such a psychology would take meaning, values, and human freedom seriously. It would be interpretive in nature, willing to make and criticize value judgments, and respectful of human responsibility. In the next chapter I shall try to lay a groundwork for such a Christian psychology by looking at the way in which regularities, meanings, and values interrelate. After exploring these themes in more detail in chapters 3 through 5, we will be in a position in chapter 6 to look at the role of freedom and responsibility in human life and in psychology, and at the importance of freedom for Christian thinking about persons. A psychology which takes meaning and values seriously will be a psychology which sees human beings as more than machines, and understands that the search for regularities in human behavior does not require determinism. In the last chapter I will return to the theme of Christian psychology, and conclude with an appeal for psychologists to see themselves not merely as Christians in a secular field, but as the psychological community within the church.

2

The Three Faces
of Psychology

In the last chapter I described psychology as still relentlessly empiricist in character. Some will undoubtedly object that this is an exaggerated and oversimplified view of the field. It ignores the incredible diversity within the academic establishment, the broad range of differences between trait psychologists, social psychologists, counseling and clinical psychologists, experimental psychologists, cognitive psychologists, and so on. Even more significantly, it ignores the often contentious history of such attempts to challenge empiricism from within the field as have been seen in movements like existential psychology, humanistic psychology, and phenomenological psychology, as well as challenges from more mainline psychologists.[1]

This objection is correct. My characterization of psy-

1. Mary Stewart Van Leeuwen cites a number of articles critical of the dominant view which have appeared in the *American Psychologist* in the last decade, including pieces by George Albee, Richard Atkinson, D. L. Bazelton, Jerome Frank, Frederick Kanfer, David McLelland, S. B. Sarason, and Roger Sperry. See her "Psychology's 'Two Cultures': A Christian Analysis," *Christian Scholar's Review* 27, no. 4 (1988).

23

chology is oversimplified, as are many generalizations. Interestingly enough, however, many of the insurgents have characterized the field of psychology in similar terms. They have felt like outsiders struggling against the dominant establishment. Curiously, they have often attempted to justify their revolt by conforming to the criteria of the establishment they are trying to dislodge; by, for example, attempting to define the "inner variables" they consider important in terms of visible, external behavior, or by arguing that their approach has led to good empiricist-style research.[2] All of this shows the power of the empiricist paradigm, even over its critics, and it shows that my oversimplification is not without point.

These disputes in psychology are invariably philosophical in character, though psychologists themselves have a penchant for calling philosophical disagreements "methodological." Both the empiricists and their opponents often characterize the arguments as centered upon the "proper path to knowledge." The dominant paradigm stresses objective observation—intersubjectively confirmable, preferably measurable, with proper controls to filter out bias. The insurgents are characterized as favoring other methods, with introspection, intuition, deductive reasoning, and common sense the most common candidates. It is a mistake on the part of the critics of empiricism to concede the realm of empirical observation to the empiricists. Doing this is like allowing extreme right-wing politicians to monopolize the mantle of patriotism. The disputes over empiricism are not disputes over the central role of observation and experience in gaining knowledge—that should be admitted by everyone. They are disputes over the nature of observation and experience.

---

2. For an illustration of this see Carl Rogers, "Toward a Science of the Person," in *Behaviorism and Phenomenology*, ed. T. W. Wann (Chicago: University of Chicago Press, 1964), pp. 109–40, particularly the "discussion" section. Also see Abraham Maslow, *Toward a Psychology of Being* (New York: Van Nostrand-Reinhold, 1968).

A mistake often made by the insurgents is linking the attack on empiricism as a philosophy of psychology to attacks on empirical research. The problem with empiricism is not that it leads to empirical research (though one problem may be that it unnecessarily restricts the kind of empirical research typically done). Converts to a new paradigm will not be won by denigrating or downplaying the significance of honest research. The real problem with empiricism is that it distorts our understanding of the nature and value of empirical research, even that research done by self-professed empiricists.

Both the value of empirical research and the shortcomings of empiricism can be clearly seen if we have a realistic understanding of what I term the three faces of psychology. Philosopher of social science David Braybrooke has argued that all of the human sciences have three basic dimensions,[3] and his analysis applies to psychology very nicely. Braybrooke terms these three dimensions the naturalistic side, the interpretive side, and the critical side. My terminology and my understanding of each of the three dimensions differ somewhat from his, but I am indebted to Braybrooke and to sociologist Richard Perkins[4] for stimulating many of the following ideas.

I would prefer to term the three faces of psychology the empirical face, the interpretive face, and the value-critical face. Each is valid and significant. None can really exist without the other two. I shall briefly describe each of the three faces and then defend the claim that the three are interdependent.

The Empirical Face of Psychology

The empirical face of psychology is the face that is most familiar and most easily recognizable. It is a face which

3. David Braybrooke, *Philosophy of Social Science* (Englewood Cliffs, N.J.: Prentice-Hall, 1987).
4. Richard Perkins, "Values, Alienation, and Christian Sociology," *Christian Scholar's Review* 15, no. 1 (1986).

shows itself when the psychologist looks for regularities, and it is a face which the psychologist shares, to a greater or lesser degree, with the other human sciences.

The economist wants to know whether an increase in the federal deficit correlates with an increase in the rate of inflation. The sociologist wants to know whether incidents of racism increase if unemployment is greater. The political scientist wants to know whether people who are economically well-off but from poor backgrounds are more likely to vote in accordance with their present economic interests or their past.

The psychologist wants to know if certain practices of child discipline are correlated with certain problematic behaviors in children. Are certain kinds of child abuse likely to be associated with certain kinds of deviant behavior? Is a certain learning style correlated with superior achievement in mathematics? Are egalitarian marriages more likely to lead to mutual satisfaction than are hierarchical marriages?

Why do psychologists want to know such things? Certainly there are many reasons, of many different types. One of the most powerful reasons for seeking such knowledge is simply that it is useful. If we want to turn out a lot of gifted mathematicians, and we know that a certain style of teaching and learning is more likely to help us achieve our goal, we have gained something of measurable value. If we want to cut down on the incidence of child abuse, and know that a certain type of parent education is effective in preventing such abuse, we have an achievement which has solid value.

It is very far from my purpose to minimize the pragmatic value of such knowledge. Nor have psychologists been shy about promoting the value of this type of empirical knowledge to government, industry, and the general public. If this pragmatic value were the sole good to be gained from empirical research, most of what is worth doing in any case would still be worth doing. However, a knowledge of empirical regularities has other significant value as well. The most important value is helping psychologists develop theories and models to help us better understand and explain human behavior.

The empiricist is likely to agree with this point because empiricism has typically linked explanation to prediction. Empirical knowledge of regularities is valuable because it enables us to predict behavior, but the same knowledge after the fact allows us to explain behavior. The tight linking of explanation to prediction is, however, one of the fallacies of empiricism. Many phenomena can be predicted with great accuracy, but cannot be explained; some good explanations can be given which would be useless for prediction. The ancient Babylonians could predict eclipses with great accuracy but had no way of explaining them. Geologists can explain why earthquakes occur but are powerless to make accurate predictions. We shall see later that a knowledge of regularities plays an important role in developing good explanations and theories, but the connection is not the simple one posited by empiricism.

The Interpretive Face of Psychology

The interpretive dimension of psychology focuses on questions of meaning. Many psychologists may not recognize the importance of meaning to psychology, but I shall try to show, in chapters 3 and 4, that taking meaning seriously is a precondition for quality research and practice in psychology. It is not easy to say what it is to look upon human actions as possessing meaning. The question of the meaning of "meaning" is itself one of the most vexing issues in the field of philosophy. Here we shall merely introduce the concept and hope for a fuller account in chapters 3 and 4.

Everyone can probably recall an elementary-school teacher who reprimanded students for errant behavior by asking, "What is the meaning of this behavior?" To take a less threatening example, it is not uncommon to ask, "What did he mean by doing that?" in response to an interesting but puzzling tale about someone else's behavior. In a dating situation a person may be intrigued by the question of meaning: "Did that look *mean* anything?" A person undergoing therapy is habitually late for the sessions. Does this tardiness *mean* anything?

In all these situations our attention is being called to the fact that human behavior, like a written text, can mean something. The primary or core component of meaning is the notion of "aboutness." A written text is in one sense a collection of letters or even marks on paper, but if it possesses meaning it is not merely that; the text also signifies something else which it is not. Human actions have a similar power. They are in one sense bodily movements, but like a written text they are in some sense about something. They have the power of signification.

When we deal with the phenomenon of meaning, then, we always have to deal with at least two things: a text or text-analogue and what the text or text-analogue signifies or is about.[5] The relation between the text or text-analogue and what is signified is not easy to characterize, but the text or text-analogue must be seen as an attempt to articulate, in a concrete and particular way, the meaning—which is more abstract, more universal, and in principle capable of being expressed in more than one way. To ask for the meaning is typically to ask for an account of the relationship; it is to ask how the text or text-analogue expresses the meaning. Such an account is essentially an attempt to express the meaning in a new way; it is an interpretation. Inherent in the notion of interpretation, then, is the possibility of rival interpretations, since meanings are the kind of thing which can be articulated more than once.

5. See Charles Taylor, "Interpretation and the Sciences of Man," in his *Philosophy and the Human Sciences* (Cambridge: Cambridge University Press, 1985), pp. 15–57.

What do human actions mean? What are they about? What is the nature of this particular kind of "text"? There is no one thing which human actions signify, and the request for an account of human behavior is not a request for one simple kind of story. There are many possible things to consider in order to tell the story one needs to tell when asked about the meaning of a human act. However, often the meaning of an act is bound up with its motivation; a request for meaning can be a request for the reasons for an action. To understand the reasons a person has for an action one must know something about the beliefs and goals of the agent. Closely related to these concepts are the concepts of intention and purpose.

The story which we tell about the meaning of an action presupposes that what people do and why they do what they do are heavily shaped by how they think of their actions. Persons do not usually act blindly or instinctively. Even behavior which we refer to as "impulsive" is usually behavior in which the person has some idea about what he is doing, and it is behavior which would not be engaged in if the person had a radically different understanding of the behavior in question or the situation in which the behavior is carried out. So generally an action is not understood merely as an individual act, but as an act of a particular type.

This allows persons to consider and assess various courses of action in terms of principles, rules, or policies.[6] Even the simplest of actions can be considered in this light. Last week I went to have my teeth cleaned and examined. In so doing I followed the principle of having regular dental check-ups, a rule which I absorbed at an early age, and one which the dentist's drill taught me the frightful consequences of ignoring. Rules are important to human life because, within limits and with some exceptions, human beings want to be reasonable and consis-

6. The discussion of rules which follows owes much to Peter Winch, *The Idea of a Social Science* (New York: Humanities Press, 1958).

tent in their behavior. Becoming a part of a culture is a matter of learning to follow countless rules, formal and informal, to which most members of the culture conform. Such rules are employed both for guidance and for justification. If my behavior is questioned, my first line of defense will be to cite the principle or policy which I think of myself as following and which helps to justify the behavior.

A key element in the interpretation of human behavior will therefore be a knowledge of the rules human beings follow. If I see people methodically pacing up and down in a field, I do not really understand the behavior until I know how they conceive of their action. Suppose I am told that they are worshiping God. Now some understanding of the behavior begins. But I do not really understand this behavior until I know the rules or principles behind it. The behavior makes more sense, for example, if I know that these people believe that God has commanded all human beings to periodically pace five hundred steps in an open field as an act of reverence for the God who made all open spaces and gave human beings the power to walk. When we understand the rule they are following, we understand the behavior. To generalize, a full understanding of human action requires an understanding of the rules which human beings consciously or unconsciously follow or fail to follow, and the concepts, embedded in those rules, which human beings employ to understand human actions.

It is characteristic of empiricism to try to reduce rules to regularities. If this reduction succeeds, then it might appear that interpretive psychology will be reducible to empiricist psychology. However, though rule-governed behavior is usually regular, a rule is more than a regularity. There are two significant differences.

The first concerns the normative dimension which rules possess. The difference is one which is brought out clearly in Immanuel Kant's distinction between action which is in accordance with a rule and action done out of respect for a rule.[7] Kant wanted to argue that much human behavior which conforms to moral principles is not moral in a deeper sense, because the people engaging in the behavior do not really care about morality. He had in mind the shopkeeper who is honest only because he is convinced that it is good business; if the shopkeeper thought he could cheat people with impunity he would do so. Such behavior may conform to moral rules, and thus could be described as moral if rules were simply regularities, but it is not genuinely moral because the behavior in question is not engaged in, one might say, out of respect for moral rules.

I do not wish to get sidetracked at this point into a discussion of the merits and demerits of Kantian ethics. One may rightly object that Kant's moral psychology was deficient in overemphasizing the place of rules in the moral life and overly limiting in its view of legitimate motivations for moral behavior. The point remains that there is a difference between behavior which is merely accidentally in accordance with a rule, moral or nonmoral, and behavior which is in some way significantly influenced by a rule.

Most human behavior—certainly most significant human behavior—is rule-shaped in this latter way. The clearest cases are of course explicit rules: driving fifty-five miles per hour because that is the speed limit; submitting a time card on Fridays because the rules say one must do this to receive a paycheck; coming in to see one's advisor because the college rules say one must do that in order to register.

Somewhat less clear are the myriads of implicit rules that govern social interactions. A woman chooses to wear a certain type of dress to the office because there is an

7. See Immanuel Kant, *Groundwork of the Metaphysic of Morals*, trans. H. J. Paton (New York: Harper and Row, 1964), pp. 64–67.

implicit understanding that certain types of dresses are essential to be taken seriously as a businessperson. A young person wears an earring of a particular type in one ear to indicate his willingness to identify with a certain group in the high school, and to indicate his disdain for another. A middle-aged man drives a BMW to indicate both that he is financially secure and that he is a person of discernment and judgment.

Many of these implicit rules have never been explicitly formulated, and do not need to be. They are clearly understood by the parties who need to understand. In some cases the rules may be unclear, and the actions may even conform to contradictory rules. In all these cases there is a normative dimension: a person (or group) must act in a prescribed way to attain a certain goal.

The normative dimension distinguishes a rule from a mere regularity because it brings the concept of choice or decision to the forefront. Rocks and trees and planets are regular in their behavior, but they do not make decisions about rules. A rule which prescribes how I ought to behave is a rule which I may decide to disobey. This means that rule-shaped behavior which falls short of being strictly regular may still be significant. Behavior which does not conform to a rule may still be partly explained by the rule, as when a protester walks into a space because the space is marked "No Trespassing."

In addition to the normative dimension of rules, there is one other significant way in which they differ from mere regularities. There is a close connection between understanding a rule and understanding the concepts which one would employ to articulate the rule. This connection is so close that it can be argued that understanding a rule and understanding the concepts surrounding the rule are really one and the same. For example, someone who understands the countless rules which govern what it means to be a friend understands the concept of friendship. Conversely, someone who really understands the meaning of "friend" implicitly understands the rules which govern the inter-actions between friends, even if that person might have some difficulty explicitly stating those rules if asked to do so.

Now one might argue that rules and regularities are alike in this respect, since to know that a regularity applies, one must also be able to grasp concepts. Nevertheless, there is a significant difference. A regularity of the sort which empiricism ideally seeks is readily identifiable; the ideal is some type of laboratory measurement or mechanical device to register that the regularity has occurred. However, it is an essential feature of the rules which shape human action that they must be interpreted.

One might think that some rules are so vague that they hardly count as rules. Think of the father, for instance, who tells his five-year-old son to "be a good boy this afternoon at the birthday party." What is he telling the son to do? Obviously, he is not prescribing or proscribing any particular action. The instructions are somewhat vague. On reflection, we can see that vagueness of this sort is present to a degree in almost all of the rules we follow in our daily interactions. The rules are always open-ended and can never anticipate all the possible situations in which they will have to be applied. Following a rule is a matter of interpretation.[8]

One could have rules for interpreting the rules, of course, and at times we do have such rules. But these rules in turn must be interpreted, and in the great majority of cases we do not have such rules for interpreting the rules. Human life itself can be seen as a continuous process of interpretation then.[9] The vagueness which makes life it-

8. That following a rule is not simply a matter of following another rule is a central theme of Ludwig Wittgenstein's *Philosophical Investigations*, 3d ed., trans. G. E. M. Anscombe (New York: Macmillan, 1968).

9. Charles Taylor has developed the notion that human beings are "self-interpreting animals." See his essay of that title in his book *Human Agency and Language* (Cambridge: Cambridge University Press, 1985), pp. 45–76.

self an interpretive process inevitably infects any attempt to observe and describe human life. There must then be an ineradicable hermeneutical element in psychological observation, and this will have its impact at the level of theory as well.

Imagine that a young man has committed suicide. He has appeared in front of the White House in Washington carrying a sign protesting American support for the Contras in Nicaragua. Suddenly, he pours gasoline over himself and lights a match.

What has he done and why has he done it? On the surface it looks easy enough to say. He has committed suicide, and has done it as an act of political protest. But suppose more information surfaces. The young man's father is a high government official involved in setting policy in Central America. It is disclosed that the father abused the son when the son was young, and that the son was full of anger and resentment. Further investigation shows that the son was deeply depressed, had been hospitalized, and suffered from insomnia. Additional information suggests new possibilities as we think about what was done and why. As the process of reflection unfolds, it becomes clear that the question of what act was performed is logically linked to the question of why the act was performed.

The answers may be complex, and it may be difficult or impossible to determine the truth. However, to the extent that it is possible to give an answer, the procedure of discovering the truth will include a prominent hermeneutical dimension. No matter how many facts are discovered, the primary task will be to interpret those facts, to weave a coherent and convincing story.

There are strong analogies here to the interpretation of a literary text. The best interpretation will be one which is consistent with known facts, but also illuminates little-noticed details and makes it possible to view seemingly disconnected phenomena as forming a meaningful pattern. One begins with an overall interpretive stance and tests its power to do these things by comparing it with rival interpretive stances. To a certain degree the enterprise is circular, since the meaning of particular phenomena is somewhat dependent upon their relationship to others, and different facts will take on different meanings in different configurations. But the process is not completely subjective. Some interpretations do make more sense than others, do make possible new insights, and do offer less violence to the facts as we recognize them.

Psychologists may well recognize the significance of such an interpretive enterprise in clinical contexts, but wonder whether such a subjective enterprise has any role to play in experimental contexts. I hope to show in what follows that the interpretive face of psychology, once one has an eye for it, can be seen just about everywhere.

The Critical Face of Psychology

Empiricist psychology prides itself on its value-free stance. Though empiricists have cheerfully admitted the fundamental importance of values when psychological knowledge is being applied, they have insisted that gathering knowledge itself is a different sort of affair. Enlightened empiricists have recognized the impossibility of a truly value-free science, but they have usually insisted that the values which are at work in science are scientific values, such as the value commitments to truth, to objectivity, to taking seriously the work of others, and so on.

Taking the hermeneutical side of psychology seriously opens the door to seeing psychology as value-laden in a much more basic way than the empiricist can allow. The message which feminist, Marxist, and other radical psychologists have been preaching is one which needs to be heard.

Since the rules which human beings follow in life have

a normative dimension, the observation and interpretation of the rules cannot be value-free. One might think that psychologists could simply describe the rules which people follow, without making any value judgments themselves about the adequacy of the rules. In certain contexts, something like this can be done, and is a valuable undertaking. Indeed, this is precisely what some phenomenologists feel psychology is all about.

The difficulty with this view is the assumption that the rules which people follow are perfectly transparent to them. One of the troubling aspects of rules, and part of what distinguishes them from mere regularities, is that their vagueness allows many different actions to be understood as following from a rule. It is equally true that the same action can be interpreted as expressing more than one rule. The question of which rule is relevant to a particular act is often a vexing one. Is a businessman who opposes raising the minimum wage really concerned about a resultant increase in the unemployment rate, or the resultant decrease in his profits? Is he following the rule "Be concerned for the welfare of those who have less than you," as he claims, or is he following the rule "Maximize the return on your investment"? Is a client who is concerned about making someone else happy committed to the rule "Love your neighbor as yourself" or the rule "Everyone must like me or I'm a worthless person"?

Settling questions of this sort inevitably leads to assessing the adequacy of the rules at issue. Are people who favor raising the minimum wage and believe that this is a policy which should be favored by those who wish to show compassion for those less well-off, foolish and misguided do-gooders? Are people who oppose raising the minimum wage on the grounds that it will raise unemployment cynical seekers of profit? Is loving your neighbor a hypocritical expression of a pathological need to please others? Part of what is needed to answer these questions is an assessment of the adequacy of the rules in question.

Someone who thinks that a particular rule is grossly or ludicrously irrational is likely to think that a proponent of the rule can fail to see this only because the proponent is blinded by self-interest. On the other hand, if we judge that a particular principle is one which a reasonable person could hold, then even if we judge it incorrect, we are likely to accept the claim that the rule is part of the explanation of the other person's behavior.

Interpretive psychology therefore will necessarily be a value-critical psychology. Psychologists who wish to understand the concepts people employ, and the rules expressible in those concepts, in order to comprehend their behavior will necessarily also ask questions about the adequacy of those concepts and rules. Are the rules people consciously claim to be following the real governing factors? Who makes the rules and sets up the sanctions which underlie many observable regularities? Whose interests are being served?

For example, are the rules, implicit and explicit, which govern the social roles of "wife" and "mother" exploitative of women and do they tend to legitimize a sexist society? Or, to look at a similar issue from a very different value perspective, do the rules which govern the role of "liberated woman" function to disrupt a stable social order by undermining the family? As these examples show, it is not possible to ask questions about the adequacy of meanings and rules from a purely neutral perspective. Inevitably, what seems reasonable or unreasonable to us will partly depend on our own beliefs about what is worth having and doing, as well as what counts as effective means for getting or having.

A clear illustration of the close link a value perspective has to the concept of rationality in psychology can be found in the work of Albert Ellis and his Rational-Emotive Therapy. Ellis deserves credit for seeing how crucial the concept of rationality is in psychology, though one could hardly find a more naive concept of rationality itself than Ellis's.[10] Ellis operates with two distinct, and possibly even competing, notions of rationality. Sometimes he speaks of rational beliefs as those which are likely to be egoistically satisfying to the agent, those which will help the agent survive and satisfy as many preferences as possible. At other times Ellis views rationality as regulating one's beliefs by the positivistic canon of verifiability; thus beliefs in absolute moral prohibitions are for Ellis irrational because it is not possible experientially to show they are true.

With these criteria of rationality in hand, Ellis proceeds to analyze human behavior. Suppose I am a devout Christian who is married to someone who is uncaring and inconsiderate, but I believe that I ought to persevere in the marriage because I believe that marriage is a divine sacrament. From Ellis's viewpoint such a belief is irrational by both of his criteria, and thus pathological. As a therapist his job is to correct my irrational thinking. I assume that if Ellis were more theoretically-minded he would find it extremely interesting to discover the causes of such pathological behavior. Behavior which conforms to Ellis's criteria of rationality, on the other hand, is seen by Ellis as hardly needing explanation at all. Since Ellis sees my own beliefs that marriage is a sacrament and that I ought to persevere since this is God's will, which explain my behavior to my satisfaction, as pitifully irrational, he can hardly do otherwise than to discount my understanding of my behavior and substitute some other.

One might think that the clearest examples of value-critical psychology would be Marxist and feminist psychologies,[11] and these are excellent cases. However, Ellis

10. See C. Stephen Evans, "Albert Ellis' Conception of Rationality: How Reasonable Is Rational-Emotive Therapy (RET)?" for a fuller version of this critique, in *Review of Existential Psychology and Psychiatry* 19, nos. 2 and 3: 129–35.

11. For an example of a Marxist psychology, see Phil Brown, *Toward a Marxist Psychology* (New York: Harper and Row, 1974). Probably the best-known example of feminist psychology is Carol Gilligan's *In a Different Voice:*

is closer to the psychological mainstream, as behaviorism edges closer to cognitivism. Ellis is simply more transparent than some other psychologists, both in the significance he recognizes in the concept of rationality and in straightforwardly affirming what he thinks rationality really amounts to.

The same themes are present, in a more surreptitious fashion, in Freudian psychology. How is Freudian psychology a value-critical psychology? Freudian psychology has an account, more or less self-consciously held by different psychologists, of what constitutes rational behavior. This is in effect an assessment of the rules governing daily interaction, particularly interaction between therapist and client. Certain kinds of behavior and patterns of thinking are accepted as congruent with reality; others are interpreted as disguised expressions of infantile wishes, hidden aggressive impulses, and so on. (Of course some behavior might be both; still, the point is that part of the reason for seeing certain behavior as the expression of hidden wishes is clearly its irrational character.)

Of course some Freudians claim to see all behavior as expressing such hidden impulses, but this stance is never consistently and universally held. No one would think that interrupting a session of therapy because the building is on fire would be an expression of "resistance." This is because it is judged rational to leave a burning building. No hidden explanation is needed. Refusing to leave a burning building would, however, be behavior that suggests a need for explanation in terms of hidden factors.

The judged adequacy of the rules and meanings the patient is operating with is surely one of the relevant factors in deciding which behaviors and patterns of thought to classify as rational and ego-autonomous and which to classify as irrational and perhaps in need of a depth explanation. These judgments arise frequently in the thera-

Psychological Theory and Women's Development (Cambridge, Mass.: Harvard University Press, 1982).

peutic situation, but Freud himself was not shy about
making such judgments about society in general, as evi-
denced by his theories about religion. Freudian psychology is not at all unique in making such value-critical
judgments about human behavior.

The Interdependence of the Three Faces

What I wish to show is that each of the three faces of
psychology—empirical, interpretive, and value-critical—
is legitimate, and that each is dependent on the others.
We have enterprises that are not only mutually comple-
mentary but also mutually indispensable.

My ultimate aim is to show the possibility and viability
of a distinctively Christian psychology. The chief barrier
to this is, as we have seen, the empiricist picture of psychology as an objective, value-neutral affair, which is
properly modeled on the natural sciences, or at least on
a certain picture of the natural sciences. The empiricist
is likely to see and emphasize the importance of regularities in psychology, but to deny, minimize, or even completely ignore the significance of the other two faces. So
in the remaining chapters, I intend to concentrate on
showing how empiricist psychology is dependent on
and in fact engages in interpretive and value-critical
psychology.

Before focusing on that task, I wish to say a few things
about the necessity of regularities for interpretive and
value-critical psychology. This is necessary because some
proponents of a humanized psychology, reacting against
what they perceive as the imperialism of the empiricists,
have wanted to throw the baby out with the bathwater,
and have denied or minimized the significance of research
which aims at discovering regularities. This is a mistake,
and showing why it is a mistake will show the empiricist
that I am sincere when I affirm the legitimacy and value
of regularity-oriented research.

Interpretive psychologists have argued that the regularities discovered by psychology are not true laws of nature. This contention is correct; the regularities discovered by psychology lack the universality, scope, and precision of true laws of nature. However, it is no part of the interpretive view of psychology to argue that human behavior, both individually and at the group level, is generally irregular or unpredictable.

We have already noted the pragmatic value of knowing about these regularities. However, a knowledge of these regularities is also valuable in focusing attention on areas where meanings need to be explored. Suppose it is true that children raised in teetotaling families are more likely to become alcoholics than children raised in families where moderate drinking is the norm. Now it is true that from the interpretive perspective such a finding is the beginning, not the end, of psychological research, a point which the empiricist will no doubt accept as well. But the interpretivist will point out that the additional study which is needed is not simply more empirical research. We want to know why the children of teetotaling families are susceptible to alcoholism, and no research which does not take seriously the meaning of drinking within the family or the rules which govern the use of alcohol is likely to be helpful in answering the question. So interpretive questions are crucial.

Note, however, that without the empirical findings the interpretive questions cannot even be posed. The empirical findings may be only the beginning of research, but they are an essential beginning. And empirical findings may be far more than a beginning. Without empirical research it would be impossible, for example, to determine if the susceptibility to alcoholism has any biological basis or component.

The interpretivist also needs knowledge of regularities to sort out reasons from rationalizations, causally effective meanings from ideology. It is quite true, as interpretivists insist, that a regularity is not necessary for the ascription of causality, and it is also true, as empiricists themselves agree, that a causal relationship cannot be straightforwardly inferred from an empirical association. Human beings, as free and responsible agents, are capable of acting in unique ways, but these unique actions do not prevent us from understanding and explaining human actions.

The behavior of a teacher who falsifies an expense account because he is short of money may be perfectly understandable and explainable, even though his actions may not conform to any known regularity describing him or any group of which he is a part.[12] We can understand why someone who needs money might do something dishonest, even if the person does not usually behave dishonestly, and even if it is not true that most people of that type would behave dishonestly in a similar situation. The interpretivist is right in claiming that a knowledge of regularities is neither necessary nor sufficient for the ascription of a causal relationship.

This does not mean, however, that a knowledge of regularities is not helpful in making judgments about causality. In fact, such a knowledge is often crucial. People are capable of unique behavior, but they are in fact generally predictable, and a regularity is often an important part of the evidence that a certain rule a person or group claims to be following is not the true explanation of some actions. When a politician claims he is voting to help the poor, but votes only for legislation which helps the poor by helping farmers in his district, voting against all other legislation which would alleviate poverty, skepticism is in order.

This last point shows the value of a knowledge of regularities to value-critical psychology, not just to the interpretivist. Value-critical psychology is especially significant

12. The argument in this paragraph and the next draws heavily on David Lessnoff, *The Structure of Social Science* (London: Allen and Unwin, 1974), chapter 4.

to Christians because any attempt to practice psychology from a self-consciously Christian viewpoint must take very seriously the reality of sin and the human tendency to deceive ourselves about our condition. Human beings are meaning-seeking creatures, but it is not always appropriate to take meanings at face value. To use the terminology of philosopher Paul Ricouer,[13] sometimes a hermeneutics of trust is appropriate, but just as frequently a hermeneutics of suspicion is in order.

A hermeneutics of suspicion will still be a hermeneutics. Human beings will be viewed not solely as machines or as products of their environment, but as sinners, responsible individually and collectively for their plight. However, one of the awful by-products of sin is that human beings, while not ceasing to be responsible for their plight, become more machinelike, less able to deal with the damage. Self-deception and the resultant lack of clarity and insight about the self diminish the scope of rational agency. People become more machinelike, in that they are more apt to be victimized by forces beyond their consciousness, however much this inability is due to their own actions. One of the outcomes, therefore, of a Christian value-critical psychology, surprising as it may seem, is a vindication of empirical studies of human beings which treat human beings as controlled by forces external to themselves, including unconscious forces which are in one sense internal.

Neither hermeneutical nor value-critical psychology can afford therefore to ignore or slight empirical studies of regularities. The discovery of such regularities is often the starting point for interpretive inquiry and is essential in order to determine what is meaningful, responsible activity and what is shaped by biological and other non-rational factors. A knowledge of regularities also plays a

13. See Paul Ricouer, *Hermeneutics and the Human Sciences*, ed. and trans. John B. Thompson (Cambridge: Cambridge University Press, 1981), p. 34.

key role in determining what meaningful links are genuinely causal and which are mere rationalization or ideology, a key component in value-critical psychology. Finally, a Christian value-critical psychology has theological reasons for the assumption that aspects of human behavior beyond the biological can be profitably studied from a perspective which views human beings as culpable victims of forces beyond their consciousness.

3

The Hermeneutical Dimension of Empirical Psychology

In the previous chapter I argued that interpretive and value-critical work in psychology needs empirical research which aims at discovering regularities. This is important to stress, but it is even more important for my purposes to show that empirical research involves interpretive and value-critical elements, because it is the empiricist myth of neutrality and pure objectivity which is the major barrier to the project of a distinctively Christian psychology.

In this chapter I shall try to show this in three steps. First, I shall sketch some commonplace truths about the nature of human behavior, or rather of that segment of what psychologists call behavior that philosophers term actions. I shall try to show the pervasiveness and significance of meaning for actions. Next, I shall draw some preliminary inferences from these points for the nature of observation in psychology, particularly with reference to the significance of the observer's personal characteristics. Then I will try to gather evidence for this view of action

45

by pointing out how even empirical research which would like to eliminate interpretive activity is forced to recognize its importance. In the next chapter I will try to say how a psychology which takes meaning more seriously would be different in two ways: by asking how psychological training might be different if questions of meaning were regarded as central, and by looking at two issues which serve as illustrations of the manner in which psychologists trained to take meaning seriously might function.

Human Activity as Constituted by Meaning

It is impossible to overestimate the significance of meaning for human activity, because human actions are literally constituted by meaning. An action is the action it is because of the meaning it possesses. Many psychologists, especially those influenced by behaviorism, will deny this claim, but I believe it can be shown to be true. In fact, the failure to recognize this truth ultimately undermined behaviorism.

The only exceptions to the principle that action is constituted by meaning are cases of behavior which are the limiting cases of true action: simple biological reflexes and perhaps some cases of instinctive behavior in young children. With these exceptions, what a person is doing at a particular time is dependent on the meaning of what he or she is doing.

Certainly an action of a particular type cannot be identified with a particular bodily movement, or even with a range of bodily movements. The simple fact is that the same bodily movement can in different circumstances be many different types of actions: the same type of action can be carried out by an indefinite number of different bodily movements. A woman who raises her arm may be voting, doing aerobic exercise, striving for recognition, protecting herself, or just stretching to wake herself. A man who pats another man on the back may be expressing friendship, condescension, or sympathy, or making a sexual advance.

One might object at this point that these are not really cases of different actions, but simply cases where the same action carries a variety of meanings, thereby showing that an action can be identified apart from its meaning. After all, in all the examples the woman raises her arm, and the man pats another man on the back, and these seem to be identifiable actions.

This objection is helpful because it illuminates the possibility of minimizing the importance of meaning through divesting human behavior of its significance. Meaning is less crucial for a psychology that deals with hand raising than a psychology which deals with voting, but a psychology which deals with hand raising is not a very interesting psychology. It does not pick out human actions as the actions which spark our interest and concern.

In any case there is no real escape from a realm of meaningful actions to a realm of meaningless bodily movements. Even hand raising and back patting represent conceptual possibilities, something one might intend to do or avoid, and thus they clearly possess meaning. Describing actions in such truncated ways does not really escape the world of meaning, but simply takes refuge in easily ascertainable meanings, meanings about which there is likely to be overwhelming agreement. However, it is important to recall the frequent price of the refuge: the trivialization of human behavior.

If the same piece of bodily behavior can be many different actions, it is even more obvious that many actions can be carried out by many different bodily movements. The woman who votes by raising her hand may, under different circumstances, vote by marking a piece of paper, pulling a lever, uttering a word, standing, or shouting. The man who expresses sympathy by patting another on the back may do the same thing by writing a note, offering to

do an unpleasant job, or sitting quietly with someone who
is suffering.

What is a meaning anyway? What am I talking about
when I refer to the meaning of actions? It is important to
see that a meaning is not to be identified with a thought
or conscious event occurring in someone's head. To say
that actions are constituted by meaning is not to say that
people must be thinking certain things for actions to be
the actions they are. People perform many actions auto-
matically or routinely, without thinking about them at all
in any conscious way. And people are often genuinely ignorant or confused about which action they are performing.

In chapter 2, I gave a preliminary description of the
concept of meaning in terms of "aboutness" or significance; to have meaning you must have a text or text-
analogue and something signified by the text. As I noted
there, it is essential to see the meaning as more universal
and abstract than the text or text-analogue which is the
bearer of the meaning. Interpretation is made possible by
this, since to give an interpretation is to attempt to articulate the meaning again.[1] The point I wish to drive home
here is that it is precisely because meaning is a universal
of this type, the kind of thing which can be expressed
again and again in a plurality of ways, that it cannot be
identified with a particular, datable conscious event. This
implies, as we shall see, that a psychology of meaning is
not necessarily oriented toward introspection of inner
events.

This is not to say that actions would have meaning in
a world which lacked consciousness. The situation with
respect to actions is similar to the situation with respect
to a written text. Such texts have meaning, and the meaning cannot be identified with an event inside a reader's

1. See Charles Taylor, "Interpretation and the Sciences of Man," in *Philosophy and the Human Sciences* (Cambridge: Cambridge University Press,
1985), pp. 15–57, for a fuller statement of this point.

head. The meaning of a text has a certain public status; the text is there for all to interpret, and thus its meaning cannot be seen as a hidden element in someone's stream of consciousness, even the stream of consciousness of the author of the text. Nevertheless, it is implausible to think that texts with meaning would exist without conscious authors and readers.

In a similar way, the meaning of an action normally has a certain public status. If I raise my hand to vote, the meaning of my action lies accessible to all who share an understanding of the life-forms of my culture; the meaning is not simply an event in my own consciousness. Nevertheless, it is essential to the meaning of an action that it be the sort of thing one could consciously intend. I may vote without thinking about what I am doing, but if I am asked, I can usually say, "Yes, I intended to vote."

Observing Meaningful Behavior

If human actions are constituted by their meaning, then observing human behavior is a more complex procedure than might be first imagined. In order to understand someone's actions, one must do more than see his bodily movements; one must perceive the meaning of what is being done. Of course in the case of familiar behavior in our own culture we do this all the time with no particular difficulty; that is why the empiricist attempt to minimize the importance of interpretation is as successful as it is. Still, though no conscious process of interpretation goes on in such cases, observing human behavior still involves something like an interpretive judgment. This becomes transparent as soon as we confront behavior we do not immediately understand, such as bizarre behavior in our own culture or behavior in an alien culture.

How are we able to make such interpretive judgments? There is nothing magical about it; it is done through ordinary experience and requires no special intuition. In growing up in a culture we learn that certain kinds of behavior in certain contexts have certain meaning. Raising your hand at a certain point in a certain kind of meeting constitutes voting.

One problem which making such judgments raises is that the judgments we make about any particular action seem to presuppose others we have already made. This is often called the hermeneutical circle, and it is a familiar issue to literary critics and biblical scholars. I see that someone is voting at a committee meeting, because I know that when people raise their hands at such a meeting at a particular time, the act is an act of voting. There is a rule, implicit or explicit, to be followed, and I understand this rule. But of course my ability to apply this rule and recognize the act of voting presupposes that I have already recognized the meeting as a committee meeting, and that I understand the meaning of the chairperson's request that all who are in favor of the motion will please raise their hands. So I can recognize one meaning only by virtue of already having recognized others. How do we break into this hermeneutical circle? The brief answer is that we do so by having learned how to live as a part of a human community.

The point I wish to stress here is that we learn these things in the course of learning how to live, not simply by gaining information and certainly not simply by carrying out observations.[2] We could not in fact carry out any observations of human behavior if we could not already make some judgments of this sort. We learn about meanings in the process of learning how to act, in the process of becoming a part of a human community. Later, to the extent that we are able to understand people who are very different from ourselves, particularly those who are from

2. See Peter Winch, *The Idea of a Social Science* (New York: Humanities Press, 1958) for detailed arguments for this point. The following paragraphs draw on Winch's ideas.

very different cultures, we do so by imaginatively extend-
ing.our world, trying to understand what it would be like
to be someone like the person we are trying to understand.
I believe, in fact, that it is partly the lack of a cross-cultural perspective that has made psychologists overlook the
importance of meaning. This leads to the hope that the
increasing importance of cross-cultural psychology will
help overcome the problem.

The connection between meaning and participation in
a form of life implies certain limitations on our ability to
understand others' behavior. A human action is a possible
way of being, and to the extent that I do not understand
this way of being, I do not understand the action, even if
I can successfully label it. This kind of understanding does
not consist simply in knowledge of facts; it is rather close
to what we often term wisdom and I shall discuss it under
that name in the next chapter.

Imagine an extraterrestrial who has no acquaintance
with religion visiting earth and observing a group of
Christians having morning devotions together, praying on
their knees. If the extraterrestrial observes this activity
over a number of days, he may be able to attach a label
to it and consistently apply the label. (Perhaps he calls it
"morning knee exercises.") But the alien hardly understands the behavior without understanding a host of other
things, such as God and our relationship to God, faith,
devotion, obedience, authority, and so on. And he cannot
understand these things without getting some feel for what
it would be like to be a Christian. He does not have to
share the Christian way of life, but he must at least be
able to enter this way of life in his imagination.

All this implies that there is a profound difference between observing events in the nonhuman natural world
and observing human behavior. Of course, in the case of
the nonhuman world we can observe things by applying
concepts to them, and these concepts have meaning as
well. But we clearly understand that the objects we ob-

serve exist independently of these meanings. Lightning was lightning long before there was any human concept of lightning. But prayer can be prayer only when people have something like a concept of prayer. Here the meaning of the event is essential to the reality of the event in a way which is not the case for the nonhuman world.

If this is correct, then there is a close link between the character of my own being and my ability to observe certain kinds of behavior accurately. My ability to recognize moral behavior may be dependent on the extent to which I have actually acquired wisdom and entered the moral life myself, or at least on my ability to understand what it would be like to do so. Even to do this in my imagination may require certain character traits or experiences. For example, it may require me to know what it would be like to be tempted to do wrong, and this may require me to have a sense of duty as something that may conflict with desire.

For human actions, in a much more profound sense than for other natural events, there are no immaculate perceptions. The observer has a critical contribution to make to the observation, and her own skills, attitudes, values, beliefs, and experiences heavily shape how and what she sees. One person who saw this very clearly was Søren Kierkegaard. He emphasized the role of the subjective participation of the observer in carrying out observations:

> What one sees depends on how one sees. This is because all observation is not merely a receiving, a discovery, but also a creation, and to the extent that it is this latter, the decisive factor becomes how the observer himself is. . . . To the extent that the object of the observation is part of the external world, the condition of the observer is a matter of indifference, or, rather, that which is essential to the observation does not concern his deeper being. On the other hand, the more the object of observation belongs to

the world of spirit, the more important is the state of the
innermost being of the observer.[3]

This means that the condition of the observer must not be
seen simply as a possible set of biases which will distort
the observations. Such bias is indeed possible, but at times
the condition of the observer is an essential enabling condition which allows the true meaning of the behavior to
be revealed.

Examples of this positive bias are not hard to find. All
of us are acquainted with the negative bias which pro-
duces reductionist accounts of the religious life by people
with no understanding of the meaning of the religious
life. Or we could think of the cynical, suspicious reporter
who cannot accept the devotion and altruism of the saint.
The paranoid who perceives the friendly attempts of others
to help him as sinister is simply an extreme example of
the way personal qualities may distort our experience of
others. The often unnoticed reverse of this is that just as
some qualities may distort or bias observation, so others
may be necessary to grasp what is observed in its fullness
or wholeness. Just as a lack of feeling for the religious
life can produce a truncated, reductionist account of the
religious life, so a person with deep religious sensitivity
may produce an exceptionally sensitive, profound account.

We can see then that a psychology which takes meaning
seriously will be a psychology which puts a good deal of
emphasis on the personal qualities of the psychologist. To
some degree this Kierkegaardian insight is recognized in
psychology, particularly in clinical training programs
which stress that the analyst must undergo analysis. But
it is a recognition which is in tension with the often-
prevailing model of the scientist-practitioner, which does
not pay a lot of attention to the moral and spiritual char-

3. Søren Kierkegaard, *Edifying Discourses*, vol. 1 (Minneapolis: Augsburg,
1943), p. 67.

acter of the scientist. And this kind of personal character development is also crucial for nonclinical areas of psychology, including experimental research.

The Place of Meaning in Empirical Studies

If meaning is as pervasive as I maintain, one might ask how empiricist psychologists have managed to pay as little attention to it as they have. Although there are cries for a hermeneutical approach to psychology,[4] those cries are clearly coming from the periphery. My answer to this objection is that it is not true that empiricists have managed to avoid questions of meaning; empirical studies are shot through with hermeneutical assumptions and claims. My criticism of empirical studies is not that the hermeneutical dimension has been ignored, because this is impossible. It is that the importance of this interpretive dimension has been downplayed, and that as a result, certain issues are ignored, treated too swiftly, or treated unclearly. (I hasten to add that these criticisms do not apply to all empirical studies.)

It is of course foolish and audacious for an outsider, relatively untrained in research design, to make such charges, and I am willing to be corrected. But is it possible that this is a case where the emperor, if not naked, is at least partially undressed, and is it possible that this is best seen by an outsider? In any case, let me try to back up my charge by briefly talking about the following dimensions of empirical research: the problem of definition, the problem of determining causal relationships, the problem of the validity of measurement procedures, and questions about the larger generalizability, significance, and relevance of empirical findings.

---

4. See for example Alan Gauld and John Shotter, *Human Action and Its Psychological Investigation* (London: Routledge and Kegan Paul, 1977).

The Problem of Definition

The problem of definition can be easily illustrated by
looking at the nature of anxiety. In an interesting book,
How Psychologists Do Research: The Example of Anxiety,[5]
David Dustin uses anxiety as his sample issue in attempting to help students understand the nature of psychological research. Beginning with the pioneering case studies
of Freud, Dustin looks at what is regarded by psychologists as representative, significant research on anxiety,
including studies by Willoughby, Gurin, Pavlov, Miller,
Mowrer, Solomon, and Wolpe. Dustin tries to help students
see the strengths and weaknesses of each type of research
with respect to such issues as reliability and validity, ability to infer causality, generalizability, and so on.

Now this book of Dustin's is a textbook, and a dated
one at that. Nevertheless, because it deals with an important research tradition, a look at some of its faults may
be useful in highlighting some difficulties with that type
of empirical research, particularly problems with how empirical findings are interpreted. The striking thing about
Dustin's book is that though it purports to be a summary
of some significant studies of anxiety, Dustin himself nowhere gives a definition of anxiety. Dustin realizes that
he needs to define anxiety, and attempts to do so by discussing fear. Fear, he says, "is an emotion produced by
danger."[6] He then goes on to describe what often happens
when a person is afraid: people have a pounding of the
heart, a sinking feeling in the stomach, and in extreme
cases may "run wildly about, crying, shouting, and laugh-
ing in rapid succession." This will hardly do as a definition
of fear; at most Dustin has described some things which
often accompany fear, and he has mixed this account with
evidently false claims. Fear is not always produced by gen-

5. David Dustin, *How Psychologists Do Research: The Example of Anxiety*
(Englewood Cliffs, N.J.: Prentice-Hall, 1969).
6. Ibid., p. 1.

uine danger, and it is certainly not true that "as the danger increases, so does the fear."[7]

Still, having told us to his satisfaction what fear is, Dustin attempts to say what anxiety is. The closest he comes to a definition is this: "Fear is natural in dangerous situations and so is not puzzling to us. But if these same emotional reactions occur when there is not enough danger to warrant them, these same emotions are called anxiety, and they are very puzzling indeed."[8]

One might infer from this that Dustin wants to define anxiety simply as unwarranted or irrational fear. If so, there are obvious problems. Are all cases of unjustified fear anxiety? If it should turn out that my fear about the safety of nuclear power is not rationally justified, does that mean that this fear was really anxiety all along? One may also ask whether all cases of anxiety involve unjustified or irrational fear. Suppose that I am anxious about taking a test; I have taken such tests numerous times in the past, and have always done poorly. Is my anxiety not really anxiety because it seems rationally justified?

The most fundamental questions are not raised by Dustin at all. Both fear and anxiety are described as emotions, but no account is given of the nature of emotion. Nor is it at all obvious that anxiety is simply a type of fear. The problems with Dustin's approach are by no means purely abstract and theoretical, because much of the research he goes on to discuss as research on anxiety does not appear to be relevant to anxiety at all, at least as *I* understand anxiety.

These questions are highlighted if we compare Dustin's work with another book on anxiety, one which is avowedly different in method and aims: Søren Kierkegaard's *The Concept of Anxiety.*[9] In this work Kierkegaard makes a

7. Ibid.

8. Ibid., pp. 1–2.

9. Søren Kierkegaard, *The Concept of Anxiety*, ed. and trans. Reidar Thomte (Princeton: Princeton University Press, 1980).

number of claims about anxiety which are strikingly different from Dustin's. For example, Kierkegaard differentiates anxiety from fear. Fear, he says, requires an object, but though it is possible to be anxious about something, it is also possible to have a kind of free-floating anxiety, to be anxious but to be unable to say what in particular one is anxious about. Kierkegaard also says that an emotional ambivalence is characteristic of anxiety. A person in the grip of anxiety is characteristically both attracted to and repelled by something, and the same ambivalence is present in the emotion itself; anxiety is unpleasant and yet there is something about it which makes us want to hold on to it. Kierkegaard links anxiety with choice; anxiety is for him something which is an indicator of freedom, and as such it is not necessarily bad or pathological. Nevertheless, anxiety is associated with the pathological. It is the psychological condition which makes sin possible, and sin characteristically increases anxiety.

Now I do not wish to suggest that Kierkegaard's concept of anxiety is the correct one, but rather to point out that the existence of such a radically different view calls up serious questions, not about Dustin's book, but about the whole tradition of research which he attempts to describe. One might of course suggest that Dustin and Kierkegaard disagree only verbally. Though they both use the term *anxiety*, they are talking about totally different things. This is possible, but questions still arise: What are the two things and how are they related? If Dustin and Kierkegaard have two different concepts in mind, is it an accident that the same word is used for each concept in our culture?

A convinced empiricist at this point might heartily agree and conclude that concepts like "anxiety" are not useful ones for scientists to employ. Why not stick to concepts like "avoidance-behavior," and give these concepts clear and unambiguous operational definitions? But I do not see how this maneuver helps the problem of definition

significantly. Putting aside the problems which attach to
the notion of operational definition, if we give an operational definition, we still need to know whether we have
given an accurate prescription for capturing *what we really
want to study*. Suppose the operational definition really
does measure "avoidance-behavior." The question still remains as to what "avoidance-behavior" really is. How, for
example, is it related to anxiety?

It is not likely that a study of all attempts to avoid
something will be interesting. If the psychologist tries to
cut all links with the ordinary language of action (as has
been done by some, for example, who simply define intel-
ligence as whatever is measured by IQ tests), then questions arise about the relevance of the resulting psychology
to actual human problems and behavior. If we are concerned about anxiety, then a psychology which has nothing to say about anxiety will not be very valuable.

My conclusion, then, is that the problem of definition
is a genuine problem. I do not claim that the problem is
insuperable; after all, good empirical research does occur.
I claim only that it is a problem which requires sensitivity
to and reflection on questions of meaning. Such questions
cannot be resolved simply through clever technology or
ingenious research design.

The Problem of Causation

Many empiricists recognize the problematic character
of the concept of causation, and are therefore more comfortable talking about "functional relationships." But the
concept of causation is basic to inquiry; whether the word
is used or not, people want to know what causes what.

How do empiricists in psychology attempt to discern
when a correlation represents a genuine causal relationship? So far as I can tell, there are two important methods.
One is simply to seek to determine whether the correlation is "genuine" or "spurious." The terminology is misleading, since spurious correlations are as real as any

other, but the idea makes perfectly good sense. One must try to determine whether the relationship between two variables is really functional by controlling for other variables. If the correlation is genuine, this does not establish a causal relationship, since both variables may be the effect of some third variable, but if the correlation is spurious, this suffices to rule out a causal connection.

Later, in chapter 6, I shall argue that a lawlike relationship is not necessary to impute causality in cases of human action, so I do not believe that this procedure can actually eliminate the possibility of causality in individual cases. With this exception in mind, however, I have no criticism of this procedure. We must simply keep in mind that all it does is show that in certain cases a causal relationship probably does not exist.

A second technique used by empiricists to determine causal relationships is to determine temporal order. When two variables are functionally related, the earlier one is the cause. This is also a reasonable procedure, since causes usually precede effects.

But again there are limitations. First, this procedure cannot really establish whether a causal relationship exists; it only helps in determining the direction of causation in cases where it is assumed that there is causality. Secondly, with respect to many events in nature which occur repeatedly, chicken-and-egg problems arise; it can be difficult to determine which came first. This is doubtless part of the reason psychologists find the laboratory experiment attractive, since one can usually do in the lab what cannot be done very well in survey research or natural observation, namely, determine temporal priority. However, it is hardly news that laboratory experiments carry with them problems with generalization which usually make them ill-suited to establish causation in real-world cases. Thirdly, it seems plausible that there are some causal relationships in which cause and effect are ongoing processes and occur more or less simultaneously. We see then that these two techniques, while genuinely useful, are not tremendously powerful when it comes to establishing causality.

Now how is causality established in physics? Certainly, physicists also try to discover empirical correlations, and they try to determine temporal order. However, they do more than this as well. A crucial factor in establishing a causal relationship is showing some kind of connection between two events. Suppose that a strong correlation were discovered to hold between church attendance in North America and the amount of the rice harvest in India. No matter how good the correlation, no one would be tempted to hypothesize that a causal connection exists. The reason for this is that there is no known meaningful connection between the two variables. On the other hand, no one would question a correlation between the amount of rainfall or sunshine and the rice harvest in India, because there is a well-understood connection between rainfall and sunshine on the one hand and the growth of rice. It is a basic principle of physics that, except for the most basic—and therefore mysterious—forces, such as gravity, causal connections are accepted only where it is plausible to believe that the two variables are linked through some intervening mechanism.

The same is true in psychology. If one reads research reports carefully, one comes across comments like "common sense suggests" and "it seems plausible that." These comments are a confession that certain kinds of empirical connections are recognized as causal, or probably so, because we see that there is a connection between actions of a certain type and certain ends. Human actions are intentional; they have ends, and to understand the action is to understand the end.

Recently, a controversy has arisen over the effectiveness of the detoxification centers in a county near the one in which I live. Empirical research shows that a large number of chronic alcoholics come to the centers repeatedly, and some have suggested that the centers tend to cause the alcoholics to continue to be alcoholics, rather than helping to end the chemical dependency. The reason this suggestion is plausible is that the treatment methods of the centers include giving the alcoholics a clean, warm place to sleep, clothing, and money. To the extent that we understand what it is like to be an alcoholic, we understand that these are things which alcoholics want, so we find it plausible that the alcoholics could rationally judge that a continuation of their dependency is the most effective way to attain these goals.

My point is not to downplay or minimize the value of empirical research here. Without the statistics showing the high rate of return for alcoholics, it would be hard to make a case that the treatment centers are causing a continuation of the problem. My point is rather that in making a judgment about causality, we also rely on our hermeneutical understanding of human action. We need to know what people are trying to do and why they are trying to do it. Such hermeneutical understanding is not enough by itself; as I argued in chapter 2, we must test empirically to see whether such self-understanding conceals hidden motives and rationalizes unsavory relationships. But the hermeneutical relationship is important and, in many cases, inescapable. It would be far more healthy for psychologists to admit this, even though this would be acknowledging that a crucial aspect of psychological research depends on a personal quality that cannot be ensured through attention to research techniques. For, as I have already argued, my understanding of human life is closely related to the kind of person I am, which in turn determines the kinds of persons I am prepared to imaginatively embrace as fellow human beings.

The Problem of Validity

The problem of validity is closely tied to the problem of definition already discussed but is not identical to it. The problem of definition is the problem of gaining a clear

understanding of a concept, while the problem of validity
has to do with attempts to measure the occurrence of a
phenomenon. Problems with validity often stem from poor
definitions, but it is possible to have a clear understanding
of a concept and still lack a useful tool for measuring the
occurrence of the corresponding phenomenon.

Speaking as an outsider, and therefore with the proviso
that these comments may be ill-informed, it seems to me
that psychologists are far more comfortable with questions about reliability than validity. Very sophisticated
statistical techniques have been developed to deal with
questions about reliability. My thesis is that questions
about validity are given a much less satisfactory treatment simply because such questions do not lend themselves to technological solutions. They require hermeneutical understanding.

Since I am an outsider, I was pleased to see some recent
support for my conjectures by a respected psychologist,
Donald W. Fiske. In a recent article Fiske says that "construct invalidity is pandemic" in psychology.[10] A good deal
of the problem, he says, is simply that investigators have
no clear idea of what they are looking for: "Although investigators have no trouble in labelling their target construct, all too often they stop at that point. Sometimes, a
short verbal definition is added. Rare is any account of the
essential conditions for potential manifestation of the behavior and even more rare is a full conceptual statement
of the construct."[11] I would submit that this is true because defining the essence of a concept is precisely the
kind of thing which cannot be done simply by developing
a technique. Essentially conceptual questions require reflection and are not the kinds of problems which can be
solved through more rigorous statistical work.

10. Donald W. Fiske, "Construct Invalidity Comes from Method Effects,"
in *Educational and Psychological Measurement* 47, no. 2 (1987): 286.
    11. Ibid., p. 288.

A look at a textbook designed to teach psychologists how to do empirical research shows how awkward psychologists find questions about validity. R. Barker Bausell discusses validity by dividing it, in somewhat standard fashion, into different types: content validity, predictive validity, concurrent validity, and construct validity.[12] With respect to each type, Bausell notes severe problems. Content validity, in practical terms, is usually a matter of people who know something about the field making a judgment that items on a test or survey are in fact relevant to what the test or survey aims to measure. This obviously assumes that the people making the judgment understand the relevant concept; content validity can be no better than their hermeneutical understanding.

Predictive validity is often irrelevant, since a test can be an accurate predictor of some future behavior, while completely failing to measure in any accurate way the quality it was designed to measure. Conversely, an instrument might accurately measure the existence of an attitude, for example, while failing to have much predictive value.

Concurrent validity, Bausell notes, faces an interesting dilemma. Concurrent validity tries to determine whether one measure is reliable by employing another measure as a criterion. This is a popular way of dealing with validity, since it allows one to describe validity in terms of a correlation coefficient. It is obvious, however, that the validity of the new measure is dependent on the assumption that the old measure is valid, and this type of validity is thus of no help when the question is that of determining whether any instrument is valid in the first place.

Construct validity, Bausell claims, really encompasses all the others, and therefore if there are problems determining the other types of validity, then the situation is no

12. R. Barker Bausell, *A Practical Guide to Conducting Empirical Research* (New York: Harper and Row, 1986), pp. 208–25.

better for construct validity. What I find really interesting in Bausell's study is his conclusion. In effect, he says that the whole question of validity is one psychologists should quit worrying about. Since there is no empirical method, and indeed no "method" of any kind (in the sense of a set of procedures which can be more or less mechanically followed and which are highly likely to work) for determining validity, validity is not a useful concept. Worrying about validity is like throwing dust in the air, and then complaining that one cannot see: "My conclusion, therefore, although undoubtedly antithetical to the majority of the research community, is that we have indeed raised a dust through which it is impossible to see, that the multi-faceted concept of validity is empirical research's version of the emperor's new clothes parable, and that researchers employing paper-and-pencil or observational measures follow the lead of their hard science colleagues and disregard validity."[13]

Instead of validity, Bausell urges his colleagues to worry about the utility of a concept. Perhaps he optimistically feels that in the long run measures of a construct which are useful will also be valid. Perhaps this is true. Still, we must ask, how is the usefulness of a measure to be determined? If a measure is supposed to gauge a particular phenomenon, it hardly seems possible for it to be useful unless it accurately does just this.

Saying that psychologists should ignore questions about validity just because these questions cannot be answered empirically is a reductio ad absurdum of the straight-jacket in which empiricism puts empirical research. Far more reasonable would be a recognition that here is a point where empirical research is tied to conceptual understanding, and to recognize that this kind of conceptual understanding cannot be achieved through a technique. It is achieved through living as a human being,

13. Ibid., pp. 223–24.

and through disciplined reflection and conversation on that life.

Questions about Generalizability, Relevance, and Significance

To me it seems perfectly obvious that decisions about whether research findings are generalizable require hermeneutical understanding. Generalizing from a laboratory experiment involves a decision about whether the characteristics which are crucial in causing a particular phenomenon have been captured in the experiment. This is the heart of the humanists' objection to generalizing from experiments with pigeons and rats to humans. It surely is legitimate to generalize from the lab to the real world at times, but our justification for doing so can only be a deep and thorough understanding of the actions and traits we are making inferences about.

Questions of a similar type arise for survey research. Since all such research is sample-specific, questions about whether and to what populations one can generalize always boil down to judgments about the relative importance of the ways in which the groups are similar and different. But such judgments are highly dependent on one's ability to understand the nuances of a particular form of life. To an atheist the differences between a Jim Bakker and a Billy Graham may look slight; both are television evangelists. Perhaps one can conclude that the followers of each will have similar characteristics. Someone who knows and understands both men well, and also knows their followers, may realize how vastly different the two are.

Surely, judgments about whether findings are really significant, and whether they are relevant to practical problems, are even more obviously dependent on hermeneutical understanding. Empiricist psychologists make such judgments all the time, when they decide to publish findings (or not to seek publication), when they decide they are competent (or not competent) to offer help on a certain problem, and even in decisions about what is worth studying and what is not.

My conclusion is that empiricist psychologists are in a poor position to criticize attempts at hermeneutical psychology, since they themselves are involved in hermeneutical inquiry. It is true that such inquiry is sometimes disguised, as when a measure is assigned a numerical rating of validity which is determined by averaging the numbers subjectively assigned to the measure by different raters. The apparently objective number in such a case tends to hide the fact that what stands behind the number is the hermeneutical skill of the raters.

Or, to take another example of disguising hermeneutics, the validity of a test is assessed by determining the correlation between answers to individual questions and the test as a whole; such a procedure can certainly sharpen a test, and it can certainly improve the validity of individual items *on the assumption that the test as a whole is valid.* But that assumption, of course, embodies a huge interpretive judgment, a judgment that does not have to be faced as long as one can keep busy with questions that can be handled through statistical techniques, such as the correlation between one test item and another.

I am not suggesting that psychologists should be less rigorous in attempting to measure what can be measured, or less concerned to develop techniques to do what can be done by techniques. I am rather suggesting that psychologists broaden their horizons to see that being a good psychologist, even being a good researcher, requires more than the skills of collecting data and performing operations on the data. It requires inquiry into the meaning of human actions, and such inquiry cannot be insulated from what introductory psychology textbooks often pejoratively describe as "speculation," "intuition," or "common sense."

4

Taking Meaning Seriously in Psychology

In the previous chapter, I argued that empiricist psychology is in a poor position to deny that psychology has a significant hermeneutical dimension, since empirical research involves interpretive activities, even though empiricists sometimes try to hide or minimize this fact. But how would a psychology which took questions of meaning seriously as part of its central task be different from psychology as it is currently practiced?

Note that the question is not about some alternative discipline, which would replace or complement psychology as it currently exists. In my perspective, hermeneutical or interpretive psychology is not a new enterprise, but one dimension of psychology, an essential one which also requires the other dimensions to be complete. Hence I am not asking myself to imagine a new discipline, constructed from scratch, but to imagine what reforms or changes, some of them modest perhaps, would bring the hermeneutical dimension into greater prominence.

My strategy is as follows. After an attempt to distin-

guish the quest for meaning by way of what I call "recollection" from introspectionist psychology, I shall try to
say something about the personal qualities of psychologists who would give greater prominence to inquiries about
meaning. For personal qualities are what count ultimately; no mechanical techniques or skills can do the job
here. The crucial personal quality is one I shall designate
by the traditional term *wisdom*. Next I shall make some
suggestions about the ways in which the preparation of
psychologists could be altered to foster the growth of wisdom. Finally, I shall discuss two key issues as case studies
which illustrate how psychologists with the wisdom to
think deeply about meaning might approach issues differently than is currently the case.

Introspection and Recollection

One of the first issues which must be faced in thinking
through the interpretive dimension of psychology is the
bugaboo of introspectionism. Would a psychology which
takes meaning seriously be a return to the methods of
introspection, thought by many psychologists to be discredited?

For the most part, I believe the answer is no. It is not
that I agree that introspection is a useless or discredited
technique. In fact, introspection in some form is a prominent part of the empiricist bag of research tools, mas-
querading in both experiments and survey research under
the less pejorative title *self-report*. Human beings are
usually, though not always, aware of what they are doing,
and they are often in a position to tell us things about
their actions, reasons, beliefs, and so on, which we would
otherwise be unable to know. It would be foolish to ignore
such a source of information, and psychologists do not in
fact ignore it, or at least not generally.

However, a psychology which focused more seriously on
questions of meaning would not be limited to introspec-

tion, especially not to introspection as practiced by such founding fathers of psychology as Wilhelm Wundt and Edward B. Titchener. These psychologists used introspection as a source of knowledge about psychological events and processes. As empiricists, they were looking for regularities, empirical links between psychical events and external stimuli. However, as I argued in chapter 3, the meanings of human activities are not events, internal or external, and understanding the meaning of an action cannot be reduced to introspecting some inner occurrence.

It is easy to confuse reflection on meanings with introspection because both require what might be called a first person point of view. In chapter 3 I argued that we acquire an understanding of meanings in the course of coming to understand what it means to exist as a member of a human community. Thus to understand an action is to understand what it would be like to be the agent who performs the act; such understanding requires an imaginative participation on our part. This is why interpretive understanding is conditioned by the personal qualities of the person who is trying to understand.

However, the possibilities that a person understands in understanding the actions of another are possibilities, not events. Grasping a possibility is a matter of apprehending a universal, not introspecting an occurrence. What is needed to understand meanings is more like recollection than introspection. It requires critical reflection on one's own life and the lives of others one has encountered, a critical reflection in which the relationships of various possibilities are sorted out. What is crucial is an attempt to see things together, to view life as a whole.

Psychology and Wisdom

This kind of understanding of human life is essentially equivalent to what is often called wisdom. We all know people who have a great deal of knowledge, even a great deal of psychological knowledge, who are not wise. Conversely, we all know people who seem very wise who are not up to date on the latest empirical findings. It seems plausible then that wisdom is not to be identified with an accumulation of knowledge or facts.

An empiricist might respond at this point that wisdom is indeed different from knowledge, but that science aims at knowledge, not wisdom. I cannot accept the claim that an ultimately adequate science of human behavior would be divorced from wisdom. If I am right in my argument in chapter 3 that empiricist psychology must deal with questions of meaning, then I think it follows from this that psychologists who were wise, who had the kind of understanding of human behavior that is linked with understanding of what it means to live as a human being, would be better psychologists than those who lacked this quality.

But can wisdom be taught? I have already argued that understanding is not the kind of thing which can be captured by more rigorous research techniques. Does this mean that nothing can be done to cultivate these qualities?

Certainly there are no techniques which can be employed to guarantee that trainees will acquire wisdom. For one thing, wisdom cannot be forced on anyone; just as therapists know that in many cases a client must want to change for therapy to be effective, so a person must want to become wise in order for any experiences or education to be any help toward that goal. It is by no means the case that everyone wants this kind of wisdom.

It is important at this point not to confuse wisdom with shrewdness. What the world calls wisdom is what I would term worldly wisdom, which is essentially shrewdness. The worldly-wise person knows when not to get involved, when not to commit himself, and how to manipulate situations effectively to obtain desired results. Such a shrewd person may be as foolish as that worldly-wise person who built bigger barns and stored up worldly possessions without considering that his life might be taken from him and an accounting of it required of him that very night.

Most people want to be shrewd, but true wisdom is not so immediately desirable. Really understanding human life goes hand in hand with understanding one's own life, an understanding which may be painful. But the fact that wisdom cannot be guaranteed by a technique does not imply that nothing can be done to encourage the development of wisdom. In what follows I shall sketch some of the ways wisdom can be encouraged. My hope is that some of these activities could be included in the training of psychologists, and that this would result in a broader, richer psychology, a psychology which takes meaning seriously.

I shall discuss four ways in which wisdom might be nurtured. These include training and experiences in the other human sciences (particularly history, sociology, and anthropology), in literature, in philosophy, and in what I shall call "Christian learning." As will become apparent, however, each of these areas will have to be approached in a special manner for them to be really helpful.

I realize that I am hardly the first to urge that the training of psychologists be broadened. In 1926 Sigmund Freud described the training of therapists in the following terms: "The analytical curriculum would include subjects which are far removed from medicine and which a doctor would never require in his practice; the history of civilization, mythology, the psychology of religion, and literature."[1] So my calls are not new, but they are as much in need of being heard as ever.

The Contributions of Other Human Sciences

Relations between psychology and such disciplines as sociology, anthropology, and political science have not al-

1 Sigmund Freud, *The Question of Lay Analysis* (London: Imago, 1947), p. 77.

ways been cordial. Despite, or perhaps because of, the common subject matter of human action, these disciplines have sometimes dueled for prestige and status, and all have sometimes had ambivalent relations to their older sister, history. A psychology which took meaning seriously would be a psychology which laid these cool relations to rest.

The other human sciences have, to a degree, suffered from some of the same empiricist blinders as has psychology itself, so I do not suggest that psychologists should simply sign up for courses in these areas and become apprentice sociologists, historians, and the like. One could argue, in fact, that these disciplines cannot really help, that they need hermeneutical understanding as much as psychology.

With respect to some of what goes on in these disciplines, this is true. So why am I urging their importance? Chiefly, because these are disciplines where one genuinely encounters the other. Such an encounter can play a crucial role in developing self-understanding and an understanding of other life-possibilities. The sociologist who focuses on minorities, the anthropologist who looks at alien cultures, the historian who gazes on past times—all give us ways of encountering forms of human life which are genuinely other.

One can, of course, argue that one cannot really gain an understanding of the other from the other in this direct way. Must not the understanding already be present in order to recognize the life-style one is encountering? This argument is another version of the hermeneutical circle, which is present in all interpretive enterprises. Yes, there is a sense in which a pre-understanding must exist to make it possible for me to engage the other at all. As a human being I approach the others of another culture or age with certain common assumptions about what it means to be human. I assume that the others will be concerned with birth, love, and death; that they will have families and care about them. The other is never completely alien to me.

Nevertheless, the encounter, when it is genuine, puts my pre-understanding to a meaningful test. The other can be very different from me even in being similar. He loves but does not express the meaning of love as I do. She fears death, but deals with her fears differently than I do. The encounter with the other rescues me from the age-old assumption that my ways of doing things are the only possible ways. It not only expands my world by giving me an understanding of new life-possibilities, but changes my world. My own actions and meanings look different when viewed against the relief of rival and alternative actions and meanings.

A few concrete examples will reinforce the point. One does not really understand racial prejudice until one has come to know a racist society. One does not really understand the meaning of worship until one sees the difference between the worship of a believer in the one God who made heaven and earth and the worship of a polytheist. An encounter with a traditional society can produce a keen sense of the fragmented individualism of modern, Western society. Conversely, a rigid, caste-dominated traditional society can awaken an appreciation for the opportunities and individual freedom afforded by contemporary societies.

A useful model of the kind of social science which I have in mind here is the work of Robert Bellah and his associates in *Habits of the Heart*. Though their work is grounded in empirical research, Bellah and his colleagues focus their attention on understanding the life-possibilities which give meaning to contemporary lives in North America. The characters they analyze, such as the therapist, the manager, and the entrepreneur, are representative types which focus our attention on the meaning of life. Bellah's own vision of social science as public philosophy, providing a critical and reasoned forum for thinking

about the nature of our lives together, is precisely what
is needed in hermeneutical psychology. Bellah's book could
be read with profit by psychologists, other human scientists, philosophers, and theologians as they seek to gain
a better understanding of human life.

The Contributions of Literature

It is almost a cliche among critics of psychology that
one can gain more understanding of human life from literature than from psychology. Psychologists themselves
have usually conceded that a type of understanding of
human beings comes from reading a novel or a short story.
But they have usually gone on to insist that this understanding is not the kind of knowledge prized by science,
and that whatever is gained from literature is therefore
not of much help to psychology. The usual claim is that
literature may indeed contain valid insights, but that those
insights are not scientifically validated.

It is true that literature does not give us empirical information about causal sequences, but then it is not
supposed to do that. Literature gives us insight and an
understanding of the meaningful connections between various actions. If my argument that hermeneutical understanding is essential for empirical psychology goes through,
then a more serious look at the contributions of literature
is in order.

If one's goal is a better understanding of the meaning
of human activity, one can hardly do better than to look
to the great poets, novelists, and playwrights. Where can
one go to find a better understanding of the nature of
mistrust and jealousy than *Othello*? Who portrays better
the nature of greed than Shylock in *The Merchant of Ven-
ice*? If one wants to understand the nature of racism, what
better way to learn than through the innocent eyes of
Huckleberry Finn? How better to explore the meaning of
various attitudes toward death than to experience the

dying of Ivan Ilyich? Who better helps one to understand the meaningless, trivialized life of upper-middle-class U.S. society than John Updike in *Couples*?

The special power of literature is that it does not merely communicate information, but draws the reader into a world. The reader does not merely view this world as a spectator, but identifies with the characters in it, thus making possible the kind of participatory understanding which I have argued is the basis of all human understanding. It is true that Shakespeare does not tell us what kind of conditions are more likely to produce a mistrusting or jealous personality. For that empirical research is needed. But if our goal is to understand the nature of jealousy and mistrust, and to see how they fit together in a personality, then we cannot do better than *Othello*. Shakespeare does not give us causal knowledge about these human attitudes; he gives us something more valuable: an understanding of what it would be like to be jealous and mistrustful. In doing so he holds up a mirror to us; we may discover the jealous and mistrustful aspects of our character.

Of course it is easy to see that reading great literature does not always have such an effect. The subject can be reduced to the communication of information and made as boring as any other. But I am convinced that a serious and deep exposure to great writers would produce deeper psychology. One can see this in psychologists who have a broad, liberal education and do not think of psychology simply as a body of specialized information. Surely part of the greatness of Freud was due to the ways in which he utilized his knowledge of Greek tragedy to gain new understandings of neurotic behavior.

The Contributions of Philosophy

Some psychologists will no doubt suspect a hidden agenda in my plumping for wisdom. Am I not holding out for the value of my own discipline? I am a philosopher by trade, and the very name suggests a lover of wisdom.

I am far, however, from uncritically embracing my own discipline. Too much of contemporary philosophy has become a kind of highly technical logical one-upmanship, an unedifying game which is unlikely to be of much use to psychologists. And a good case can be made that many of the problems of psychology came about not because of the divorce of psychology from philosophy, as philosophers like to think, but because psychologists were too dependent on a certain philosophy, the logical positivism which dominated philosophy of science from the 1920s into the 1960s.

So, philosophy could be helpful in developing greater understanding in psychologists, but not just any old philosophy. Philosophy must truly be a search for wisdom and a love of wisdom. Several areas of philosophy are likely to be of help.

First, a serious look at the history of philosophy should enlarge our horizons. Until the time of Wundt and William James, psychology was a branch of philosophy, and many problems, such as questions about the nature of innate ideas, perception, and the degree to which human beings are naturally social beings, are formulated clearly and debated incisively by such thinkers as Plato, Aristotle, Thomas Aquinas, Thomas Hobbes, René Descartes, John Locke, David Hume, and Thomas Reid.

A second area where philosophy can be helpful is in the philosophy of action.[2] Although I see no need for psychologists to worry about the more byzantine and scholastic elements of various theories of action, some understanding of the discussions surrounding the key concepts which bear on human action would be helpful. I mean by this

2. Much excellent work in the philosophy of action has been done. One of the finest recent books is Alan Donagan's *Choice* (London: Routledge and Kegan Paul, 1987).

such concepts as rules, purposes, reasons, intentions and intentionality, meaning, and the nature of agency itself. A psychology which is aware of these debates is at least not likely to lose sight of the fundamental importance of meaning.

A third area which could be of significant help is moral philosophy. I shall argue in the next chapter that psychology cannot and should not be a value-free endeavor. If that is correct, then a serious study of the thinking philosophers have done about human values—obligations, goods, virtues—could be of inestimable good. Of course the study of philosophical thought in this area cannot be uncritical; otherwise it would not be philosophical. Christians will be especially alert to the manner in which un-Christian ways of thinking about good and evil, right and wrong, have shaped philosophical discourse. Nevertheless, an immersion in this philosophical dialogue would give a depth to psychological discussions of such topics as altruism, assertiveness, identity, guilt, and many others.

A significant barrier to psychologists learning from philosophy is the perception that philosophical disputes are interminable. It was to get away from such never-resolved arguments as the question about whether reasons are causes that psychology declared its independence of philosophy.

It is true that many philosophical disputes are never finally resolved. This does not mean that no progress in philosophy is made. Positions are clarified; arguments are refined; and at times something like a consensus is even gained. But philosophers have a healthy suspicion of such consensus when they are being truly philosophical. One of the reasons philosophical disputes are interminable is precisely the willingness of philosophers to continually ask the basic questions and refuse to go along with the fashions of the age.

Another reason philosophical questions are not finally resolved is that many of them bear on the basic question

of the nature of human life and its purpose. To answer
these philosophical questions is to define one's own sense
of who one is. Such questions are not merely factual, and
they cannot be decided simply by accumulating empirical
information. Someone who resents the idea that he is a
creature who is responsible to the God who made him will
doubtless find certain philosophical views more attractive
than others, and these philosophical views will have grave
consequences for psychology. The continual disputes may
be frustrating, but such frustration is part of the price we
pay for sin. In any case, ignoring philosophy because of
its character will not help if psychologists inevitably take
philosophical positions. The question is not whether psychology is philosophical, but whether it will become more
self-consciously philosophical.

The Contributions of Christian Learning

For Christian psychologists, the sources of wisdom I
have just discussed are significant, but they pale in comparison with the resources provided by their faith. Indeed,
it is misleading to portray faith as a source of wisdom, as
if it were simply one alternative path. For one thing,
Christians believe all true wisdom comes from God, so
when wisdom is derived from studying other people, from
literature, or from philosophy, it still comes ultimately
from God. But even more decisively, Christians believe
that the key to wisdom is knowing Christ, who is the
wisdom of God incarnate. If these claims are true, then
Christian psychologists should have some special helps in
acquiring the kind of understanding of human life we are
discussing.

In fact, the contributions offered by Christianity toward
the attainment of wisdom are distinctive enough that they
should be distinguished from the methods I have discussed
in the preceding sections. I have talked of wisdom as the
outcome of recollection, a disciplined reflection on life as

a whole. Christian wisdom, however, is not grounded solely in recollection, which is the outcome of our natural human capacities, but is grounded in revelation, which is made possible by God's supernatural activity.

I fear that some will find such claims to be a reductio of my claims about the importance of wisdom, or the claims of Christianity to be true, or both. It may not appear immediately obvious that Christians have any special advantages in acquiring wisdom, since the antics of some television evangelists show that Christians can look as foolish as any Hollywood starlet.

The claim that Christianity can help create wisdom must not be taken as an empirical claim that Christians, as a group, are wiser than non-Christians on some psychological wisdom scale. Such a claim would be as silly as attempting to see whether high-school English students as a group are wiser than students taking mechanical drawing. Shakespeare provides resources for developing wisdom for the one who has eyes to see; so Christianity has resources, including supernatural resources, for those who have ears to hear and a heart willing to obey. This by no means implies that most people who profess to be Christians have taken advantage of those resources.

What are these resources? One significant resource is theology itself, which is even more fundamental for Christian psychology than is philosophy. Theology can of course be dry as dust, scholastic, and polemical in the bad sense. But it can also be a serious attempt to understand things whole, in the light of God's revelation. Good theology should help us see all things, including psychology, in the light of the great biblical drama of creation, sin, redemption, and eventual glorification. Though the project of deducing specific psychological theories from theology strikes me as useless and misguided, there should be many points where a keen theological mind should help the psychologist gain an understanding of the meaning of human action patterns.

Important as theology is, however, I do not have theology solely or even mainly in mind when I speak of the value of Christian learning in helping one to acquire wisdom. We must remember that wisdom as I have defined it is linked with being, and the Christian life is not simply a life of studying theology. The Christian's daily encounter with the person of Christ, as Christ is presented in the Scriptures and interpreted through the work of the Holy Spirit, is a continual source of self-insight and new insights into the meanings of human actions as well.

To take just one illustration, look at the power of the parables of Jesus. The parable of the good Samaritan ruthlessly reveals the tendency not to get involved, and the nature of genuine love, which is not a mushy sentiment but a willingness to act on behalf of the unloved and unlovely. Who has not been pierced by the sharp turn by which Jesus altered the perspective of the lawyer anxious to find out who his neighbor was so he could satisfy his moral obligations as cheaply as possible? Jesus showed the lawyer that he was asking the wrong question. Do not ask "Who is my neighbor?" for the purpose of drawing boundaries around your love. Ask, "Am I being a neighbor?"

Who can fail to see something of himself in the "righteous" older brother of the prodigal son, who bitterly resents his father's love and generosity toward one whom he sees as unworthy? Who can fail to see something of himself in the prayer of the Pharisee who is thankful that he is not like other men, or the cold criticism of Simon the Pharisee, who cannot understand a love which receives and forgives a prostitute?

God's revelation is not simply a revelation of himself; though it is this first and foremost. It is also a revelation of who we are in relation to himself. It is a revelation which may appear foolishness to the Greeks and a stumbling-block to the self-righteous, but it is a revelation which contains wisdom and power for those who are willing to see themselves in God's eyes.

Reflections on Meaning:
Two Case Studies

So what kind of psychology would be produced by psychologists who self-consciously worked at developing wisdom as well as knowledge? Perhaps one not so different from present-day psychology. There are many wise psychologists, especially among Christian psychologists, genuine individuals who have a sense of what life is all about. Nevertheless, this wisdom could be more freely brought to bear than it is on the discipline of psychology.

I wish to conclude with a couple of case studies which illustrate the value of reflection on meaning. Both are from Christian authors and reflect the power of biblical insights. Neither are psychologists, and that is intentional on my part, since it reinforces my argument that psychological training should be broadened so that psychologists could learn from those outside the guild. However, the issues addressed are central to current psychological concerns: the nature of need and the nature of self-esteem.

Walter on Needs and Wants

British sociologist Tony Walter, the author of *Sacred Cows*, has recently published *Need: The New Religion*.[3] In this book, he thinks deeply about a concept which has played a prominent role in psychology in this century, and, partly as a result of the psychologizing of society, plays an increasingly important role in society as a whole.

The concept of need carries with it an implicit message that the content of the need can be legitimately satisfied. My neighbor is materialistic and greedy—look at that Mercedes he bought. That is a luxury which he doesn't really need. My Volvo is quite different, of course. I really needed a roomy, dependable, safe car.

3. Tony Walter, *Need: The New Religion* (Downers Grove: Inter-Varsity, 1985).

As Walter points out, everyone decries the materialism of our society, yet our own purchases are never seen as excessive. Except in those rare cases where we see ourselves as indulging in a luxury (and even in those cases we say, "I really needed to indulge myself"), our spending is quite justified. "I needed those things." Or even better, "My child needed those things."

Now many of the things we need are good, and they may be quite appropriate uses of our money. The point, however, is that the language of need operates to insulate these choices from any moral or spiritual scrutiny. I don't have to ask whether that was the best use of my resources, because I was merely satisfying a need. Need operates here as a disguise. What is really a choice does not appear to be a choice at all, since I really needed a new car, or a pair of shoes. And of course if our marriage, our church, and our nation are not meeting our needs, then there is something basically wrong with our marriage, church, and nation. For why do these exist if not to meet our needs?

The pervasiveness and power of the concept of need in our society stands out clearly if we compare our culture with others. The idea that a person needs a richly satisfying sex life to be a fulfilled human being would have struck many medieval Christians as bizarre, even satanic. Very few societies would have found it plausible to think that intrinsically fulfilling work, free from drudgery and boredom, was a basic human need, one which society ought to meet for its members.

Nor is it necessary to be an ascetic in order to see the problem with needs. It is quite possible to see health, sexual enjoyment and communion, material goods, and fulfilling work as goods without seeing them as needs. The Christian can see all of these things as good gifts from the Father who is the source of all good gifts, and rejoice in them, without seeing them as essential to a full human life.

Obvious criticisms can be made of Walter's work. I am sure he is not ignorant of the fact that there are basic biological necessities for human beings to function adequately, and that a human being who does not eat adequately can suffer and even die. Ultimately, I myself do not agree with Walter that the concept of need should be discarded altogether. Something like a distinction between true and false needs can be defended. But I agree with Walter that making this distinction can be exceptionally difficult, and that the distinction can simply be another disguise which insulates our choices from critical scrutiny.

Walter's discussion should be exceptionally interesting to psychologists because of the prominence of the concept of need in many psychological theories. Psychologists have debated whether our needs are basically biological and instinctual, as Freudians think, or whether the humanistic psychologists such as Abraham Maslow are right in maintaining that we possess more uniquely human needs for self-actualization. But I do not believe they have thought deeply enough about what a need really is. What is the meaning of "need"? How do needs function in our society? To what extent are our needs a creation of a new morality, one which functions unconsciously to protect us from a different kind of morality?

As Walter reminds us, Christians would do well to ponder Jesus' life. Jesus was poor in material goods, never married, did not experience the joys of family life, and had no well-paying, meaningful job. The Roman Empire denied him the ability to express what we would term his political rights. He taught that people should deny themselves, not fulfill their needs. Yet Christians regard this person as the most complete person who ever lived. What then do human beings really need?

Kierkegaard on Self-Esteem and Despair

In *The Sickness Unto Death*,[4] Søren Kierkegaard gives a penetrating analysis of despair. He analyzes despair in

---

4. Søren Kierkegaard, *The Sickness Unto Death* (Princeton: Princeton University Press, 1980).

terms of the degree of consciousness of the despairer,
ranging on a continuum from unconscious despair to the
most intense despair, the despair of defiance, when the
despairing individual wills to be in despair and takes his
own despair as a proof of the malignancy of existence.

In one section Kierkegaard analyzes a common form of
despair, when an individual falls into despair as a result
of unfortunate circumstances or an unfavorable accident.[5]
"I was doing fine; then I lost my job and despaired." "I was
in love, and I was happy; then my lover found someone
else, and I despaired." Kierkegaard argues that such despair is deceptive. It appears that the despair is over the
loss of the job or the loss of the lover; in reality, he claims,
all despair is over the self.

A little reflection shows the meaning of the despair in
such cases to be something like this: I cannot accept the
self I am. If I were the self who still had the job, or the
self who still had the lover, I would be happy to be myself,
but the self who lacks the job or lover I cannot stand to
be. A contemporary psychologist might well say at this
point that the person in despair has suffered damage to
his or her self-esteem, and this is the concept on which I
wish to focus. What is self-esteem anyway?

Some psychologists view self-esteem as developing from
successful achievements. If someone has suffered damage
to self-esteem due to failures in his or her work-life or
love-life, perhaps the thing to do is to help that person see
that he or she is more successful at other areas; perhaps
the person is a devoted brother or sister, or a helpful member of a club. Maybe the person really is incompetent at
almost everything, in which case the need is to teach some
skills, perhaps social skills, or problem-solving techniques, so he or she can develop some self-esteem.

What is questionable about this is not that people are
good at different things and can become better at the

5. Ibid., p. 19.

things they do, but the whole notion that my estimation of my own worth as a person is tied to my achievements. Such a view is fatal to the self-esteem of the weak, the sick, and the aged, who can no longer compete with the strong, the healthy, and the young in the race for achievement.

I realize that Carl Rogers has seen this problem, and that his concept of unconditional positive regard is an attempt to address it. Indeed, this is one point where Rogers displays his Christian roots. However, the problem goes deeper than Rogers, with his flimsy concept of human beings as "organisms," can really see.

Kierkegaard puts his finger on the key point when he notes that in these cases of despair, the circumstances which appear to cause the despair are really just revealing a despair which was present all along. We all know that people can lose jobs and be unsuccessful in love. Such things happen to some people and not to others, but they could happen to anyone. In a sense such things are accidents, matters of fortune. To say that my self-worth depends on such an accident is essentially to admit that my self is built of straw. A person who despairs because of an accident has essentially been in despair all along. What is needed is a sense of identity, a sense of self, which does not tie my self-worth to what I am able to do or not to do. After all, what I am able to do or not to do in the external sense is heavily dependent on factors beyond my control.

At this point worldly cleverness comes to the rescue, says Kierkegaard, and tries to persuade one that, by being clever, one can reduce the odds that one will be unsuccessful in these ways. One form worldly cleverness might take at this point is the psychologist offering help in shoring up one's social skills or competence in solving problems. Perhaps an Albert Ellis will assure me that this or that bad event is unlikely to occur, and even if it does, it would not really be awful. However, the most basic need of the self, according to Kierkegaard, is not to become more clever and skillful at manipulating the contingencies of life which affect achievement. Nor is it to acquire a stoic indifference which regards nothing as really absolutely important. It is to discover an identity which is impervious to such contingencies, an identity which is only found in grounding the self transparently in the God who created you to be yourself.

Please do not misunderstand my point. I am not claiming that it is not a good thing to help people succeed in their jobs and in their personal relationships, or to help them develop the skills which will help them to do this. My point is that a concept like self-esteem contains enormous implications: What is a self? Where does the self obtain the worth which we would like to esteem? These are questions about the meaning of a concept, questions which cannot be answered merely by empirical research. Yet they are questions the answers to which inform and shape an enormous amount of research and an enormous amount of practical help. A psychology which takes meaning seriously will be a psychology which works hard on such questions and works hard at developing the wisdom to answer them better. It also, as I hope I have shown, can be a psychology which can and should think about these issues from a distinctively Christian perspective, and, in the course of developing psychologists, take advantage of distinctively Christian resources.

5

Taking Values Seriously in Psychology

any psychologists who might accept the claim that an adequate psychology must deal with questions of meaning will still balk at the suggestion that psychology as a science can and should incorporate critical value judgments. They will reason as follows: "It is one thing to maintain that psychology must deal with meaningful human actions, and that its knowledge must rest in part on the kind of wisdom which makes possible understanding. It is quite another thing to maintain that psychology as a science must attempt to critically evaluate those human activities it seeks to understand. Surely knowledge of what is the case can be distinguished from what ought to be the case, and psychology as a science must deal with the former. Psychologists as human beings can and ought to critically evaluate human activity, but they should not try to disguise their personal value judgments in the cloak of science."

This argument for value-free science makes good sense to most of us, but I want to argue that it makes good sense primarily because it rests on powerful but not often examined assumptions. I hope to show that those assumptions owe their power more to intellectual fashion than rational backing, and that they are assumptions which should seem especially dubious and especially suspicious to Christians. That they do not seem dubious to Christians shows how strongly the ruling ideas of the age have shaped Christian thinking in the twentieth century. What I wish to show is that wisdom, as I have described it, is not merely a matter of understanding meanings. Rather it requires a critical understanding of meanings, an understanding which involves a knowledge of values.

The Divorce of Facts and Values

The first assumption which I must challenge is the conviction that there is a logical gulf between statements about facts and statements about values. One of the bulwarks of value-free social science generally is the belief that facts and values are distinct. This belief goes hand in hand with others: Facts are supposed to be objective, while values are subjective. Facts can be agreed upon by impartial observers, while values are personal preferences which cannot be the subject of impartial agreement. Facts can be shown to be true or false by observations, while values are not empirically testable. Beliefs about facts can be rational or irrational, while value beliefs, if they can be said to be beliefs at all, are nonrational.

Our thinking about values is so heavily shaped by these assumptions that some Christians have advocated abandoning the language of values altogether, and I have some sympathy for this view. Talk of values today carries with it strong connotations of nonrational, personal preference: "Those are my values; what are yours?" The language of values seems both individualistic and subjective. Such talk is absent from the Bible. Can one imagine Abraham, Moses, David, or Paul recommending a particular course of action, then apologetically adding, "But of course that advice reflects my own personal values"?

Although the language of values may be ultimately unsatisfactory, or at least less than ideal, for expressing Christian views, I nevertheless wish to use that language in order to challenge the claim that the human sciences in general, and psychology in particular, must be value-free. I wish to use the language of values because it is the language which most psychologists employ to think about such questions. By using it, I hope to reveal how much is packed into the language which is open to challenge.

The plausibility of the belief that facts and values are logically distinct rests on various factors. Part of the support for the divorce of values from facts rests on the common-sense distinction between describing and evaluating an action. In particular cases this distinction is completely noncontroversial. Imagine the case of a third-grade student who has marked in his textbook with ink. The teacher characterizes the act in various ways: "Jimmy, you marked up your textbook." "Jimmy, you disobeyed the rules by marking up your textbook." "Jimmy, you were malicious in marking up your textbook."

What this example shows is that it is indeed possible to describe actions in ways that are more or less value-charged. In ordinary life we often find it useful to describe activity in language which is less value-charged, and to distinguish description of what has happened from evaluation of what has happened. One of the reasons we do this is that there is often more agreement about what has happened when more value-free language is used.

The human sciences are perfectly justified in following ordinary practice here. Thus, in attacking the idea that psychology is or should be a value-free science, I am not claiming that psychologists should never seek to employ concepts which are less value-charged than others; still less am I claiming that psychologists should not do what all of us do from time to time, namely, distinguish be-

tween judgments about what is in fact going on and judgments about what ought to be going on.

It does not follow from the fact that we often can and
should distinguish between judgments about what is in
fact going on and judgments about what ought to be going
on that we can or should make such a distinction in all
cases. Nor does it follow from the fact that we often can
describe behavior in less value-charged language and find
it useful to do so, that we can always do this or that it is
always useful to do this. Similarly, it does not follow from
the fact that some descriptions are less value-charged than
others that all factual descriptions are totally value-free,
or that they have no value implications or relevance.

I believe that the common-sense distinction between
description and evaluation only seems to support an absolute divorce between facts and values because we have
unwittingly bought into a naturalistic view of the world.
The most popular naturalistic view is that the world con-
sists of bare facts, and that values are only introduced
into the world when a subject turns up who has a personal
preference. The difficulty with such a world view, as C. S.
Lewis convincingly shows in *The Abolition of Man*, is that
all such personal preferences become ultimately unjustifiable and therefore in a sense arbitrary.[1] If reality in
itself is devoid of value, then no value statements about
reality can be correct, justified, or appropriate. When I say
that the mountain is beautiful, that an act of torture was
cruel and base, or that an act of selfless altruism was
noble, I appear to be saying something significant about
the mountain, the cruel act, or the selfless act. However,
if reality itself is devoid of value, this cannot be so. The
"value" is then to be located, not in the object of the judgment, but in the attitudes, feelings, or beliefs of the judge.

It is easy to see that such a view of values is antithetical
to a Christian view of reality. Christians believe that some

1. C. S. Lewis, *The Abolition of Man* (New York: Macmillan, 1965).

acts are really noble; others are really cruel. Some states
of affairs are really good—a just society, a family united
in love and commitment, a land flowing with milk and
honey. These things are good or bad because that is how
God made them; our beliefs and attitudes about them can
be correct or incorrect, appropriate or inappropriate. To
think otherwise is to adopt a subjective view of values
which ultimately leads to nihilism.

This brings me to my first criticism of the ideal of value-
free psychology, which is that it leads to moral nihilism.
Proponents of value-free psychology will hotly deny such
a charge. In their view, psychologists as scientists must
not espouse any moral views, and therefore must not espouse moral nihilism. To claim that value-free science
supports an attitude of moral indifference is a misunderstanding of the position, it will be claimed. Scientists as
human beings must still take moral stands, and many of
them are decent, committed human beings. They simply
cannot draw any support for their personal moral positions from science.

I am sure that many psychologists are indeed decent
human beings; inductively this seems plausible, since
many of the ones I know are. But that is irrelevant, since
people are often better (or worse) than their theories. And
I am not going to argue that psychologists can derive much
support for their moral convictions from psychology, though
this is sometimes possible. Rather, my concern is to show
how moral convictions can shape psychology.

The advocate of value-free science who indignantly de-
nies that his view contributes to moral nihilism misses the
point. To say that value-free science does not lead to any
particular moral view, including nihilism, because it scru-
pulously sees all moral points of view, including nihilism,
as statements of personal preference which cannot be supported by science, betrays a misunderstanding of the
sources of nihilism. Moral nihilism arises precisely when
moral viewpoints are seen as arbitrary personal prefer-

ences, ultimately unjustifiable. To the degree that the ideal of value-free science rests on this naturalistic view of values, it is committed to a pernicious view. And to the degree that value-free science itself embodies such a view of values, it contributes to the erosion of any belief in values as rooted in reality.

Perhaps a Christian defender of value-free science will reject this naturalistic way of defending the doctrine. Values must be excluded from science, not because values are unjustifiable personal preferences, but because values cannot be known in a scientific manner. Perhaps values are objective and rooted in reality, but are known through intuition, or divine revelation, or some other means, which cannot be employed in science. From a Christian perspective, this way of defending value-free science is much more workable than seeing values as unjustifiable personal preferences. However, it has its own dangers.

First, in a culture which esteems science, there is the danger that what is known through some means other than science will seem second-class. Values may begin to look like arbitrary personal preferences, if science represents assured knowledge, and values are known by some method which cannot be relied on to produce objective results, as science is alleged to do.

Secondly, to the degree that value judgments do represent genuine knowledge of the way things are, science seems impoverished if it must exclude values from its purview. Here the advocate of value-free science must be what I have termed a limiter of science.[2] But to the degree that science aims at a genuine and comprehensive knowledge of reality, why should it be limited in this way? If there are methods of discovering the value of things, why not incorporate those methods into science? The limiter of science faces a dilemma. Either reliable knowledge of values

2. See C. Stephen Evans, *Preserving the Person* (Downers Grove: Inter-Varsity, 1977).

is possible or it is not. If such knowledge is possible, why should it be excluded from science? If such knowledge is not possible, then values once more resemble arbitrary personal preferences.

In any case, the idea of value-free science is not usually supported purely on the epistemological grounds that values are known in a different manner than facts. More commonly, the plausibility of this epistemological theory rests on the metaphysical claim that values are a different kind of entity than facts. Once the idea that values and facts are two radically different kinds of entities is rejected, the major reason to believe that they are known in radically different ways is removed.

This metaphysical doctrine is not one that should have much appeal to Christians, once it is hauled to the light of day and made to face critical scrutiny. For Christians what is good, what is right, and what is beautiful are all solidly grounded in the way things are: God is the ultimate reality and his creation can truly be said to be good.

What Is Value-Free Science?

My first criticism of value-free science is that it is logically linked to a view of facts and values which supports moral nihilism. This is really a moral criticism, and one might imagine a supporter of the idea of value-free science replying that even if I am right, this does not settle the issue. For I have not shown that value-free science is not the proper approach to science, or that there is any other way. Perhaps an increase in moral nihilism and loss of faith in objective moral values is the price we must pay for scientific knowledge, part of what some social scientists call "secularization." In other words, even if value-free science does support nihilism, we might still have to engage in value-free science, if we are to have any science at all. Some might judge that the price is too high and we should not in fact have sciences like psychology if this is their cost, but others might judge the price an acceptable one, particularly if one throws into the scale the way in which the acceptance of moral nihilism might lessen the amount of moral dogmatism in a society. After living in the Ayatollah Khomeini's Iran, one might welcome a secularized society.

It is time that I defined more clearly what I mean by value-free science. What view, precisely, do I wish to attack? Let me begin by saying what value-free science is not. Advocates of value-free science are not committed to the view that values play no role in science. They recognize that values can play a role in the selection of topics for research; scientists study some things rather than others because they find those things interesting, important, or relevant to their concerns. Values are also necessary for scientific activity itself; scientists must value truth, honesty, open communication, and many other things, or they would not be scientists and would not engage in scientific activity.

The advocates of value-free science make two further claims, however, which I wish to challenge. They are committed to a thesis about the concepts employed in science, and another about the way in which theories are accepted. Scientists, according to the advocate of value-free science, must develop and employ concepts which are purely factual and devoid of value implications, to the degree that this is possible. Secondly, scientists should accept theories solely on the basis of facts, and not personal preferences.

It is these two claims that I shall criticize. I shall argue that it is neither possible nor desirable for human scientists in general and psychologists in particular always to avoid the use of value-charged concepts in framing their theories, though it may well be appropriate in particular cases. I shall further argue that it is sometimes legitimate for values to play a role in deciding which theories I shall accept, at least provisionally, and which theories I shall continue to maintain in the face of inconclusive evidence.

Should All Concepts in Psychology Be Value-Free?

The major reason value-free psychology is not possible is that facts and values are not logically divorced. Concretely, this means that many "factual," descriptive terms are loaded with value implications. Many of the significant concepts we use to describe human behavior cannot be applied without making value judgments, though these judgments are often tacit and unacknowledged. The following concepts are illustrations of the ways in which the question of whether something is an "x" are logically tied to the question of whether that something is a *good* "x": friendship, aggression, racism, obedience and authority, altruism, art, and religion.

Although there are different levels and kinds of friendship, a friend of yours is (minimally) someone who cares about you and behaves toward you in a way consistent with certain standards. To describe someone as a friend is to say that he meets certain standards of friendship. This does not mean that every friend is a good friend, but rather that the question of who really is a friend cannot be divorced from the question of who is a good friend.

The concept of aggression is generally regarded as an extremely important one, given the incidence of war and violent crime in our world. But what constitutes aggression? Aggression is usually thought of as an unprovoked attack, or an attack which is unwarranted by the actions of the one attacked. However, it is a matter of moral judgment what constitutes provocation or justification for an attack, and the newspapers show how greatly people disagree about such things. I do not see how any study of aggression can avoid taking a stand about what aggression really is, and this will inevitably involve taking a stand on the issue of when violence is unprovoked and unwarranted.

Sociologists and psychologists have done many studies

of the phenomenon of racism, studies which, I would be
prepared to argue, provide some of the strongest evidence
of the value of the human sciences. But what is racism?
What is it to be a racist? We might start by saying that
a racist is someone who discriminates unjustly against
some people because of their race, or someone who treats
some people less favorably than others because of their
race. We hardly notice the implicit value judgments that
these definitions contain, because the values involved are
so widely shared among educated people, particularly in
academia. Nevertheless, there are value judgments packed
into these definitions and they are significant. To see this,
one must put oneself imaginatively into a society which
is overtly racist, such as the one I myself grew up in. As
a boy I was taught that "separate but equal" treatment of
blacks was not unjust discrimination and was not unfavorable treatment, but rather a policy which worked to
the good of both races.

A pair of related concepts shows how strongly our values can shape the description of the same behavior. A
person who attempts to practice natural methods of birth
control, because she believes that this is the teaching of
the church, and therefore ought to be obeyed, will be described by some as obedient and thus good, but by others
as a dependent or compliant personality who does not want
to make autonomous decisions and is therefore unhealthy.
Questions about what a dependent or compliant personality is cannot be separated from questions about what
constitutes legitimate authority and questions about what
role authority should play in a healthy individual.

Attempts to study altruism and such other forms of
morally desirable behavior as kindness and compassion
raise equally significant questions of a moral nature. Such
concepts are inherently value-laden in a positive direction,
just as the concept of aggression is value-laden in a negative direction.

Less obviously value-laden, perhaps, are concepts such

as art and the artistic person. Nevertheless, these terms
are also value-laden. Any attempt to develop a psychology
of art or an account of the artistic person must inevitably
make judgments about what is to count as art, what is to
count as creativity. These judgments will have to be made
against the backdrop of some standards of artistic judgment. The standards will have to be broad and flexible to
account for the wide divergences of opinion about what is
quality art, but nevertheless some restrictions will have
to be placed on the term. Not just anything will count as
art, and to say that something counts as art, even bad art,
is to place it in a context where certain standards of evaluation are relevant, and certain minimal standards are
regarded as satisfied.

My last illustration of a value-laden concept or family
of concepts comes from the psychology of religion. Here
I think Gordon W. Allport's classical studies of religious
faith and prejudice are a model of the way values must be
employed.[3] Allport, himself sympathetic to religious faith,
was disturbed by findings that religious people were more
prejudiced than other people. It seemed likely to him that
these findings were due to imprecision in the concept of
"religious person" which the studies employed. Allport
surely believed that true or genuine religious belief would
not lead to greater prejudice. So he set out to develop a
sharper concept of religion by distinguishing between
people who were genuinely committed to their faith, intrinsically motivated by their religious values, and people
who had a more superficial commitment, whom he termed
extrinsic believers. Using these concepts, Allport showed
that religious belief was not in fact associated with prejudice in the case of intrinsic believers.

It is obvious that Allport's studies were shaped by his

3. Gordon W. Allport, *The Nature of Prejudice* (Cambridge, Mass.: Addi-
son-Wesley, 1954), chapter 28, and also *The Individual and His Religion* (New
York: Macmillan, 1957), p. 59.

values here. His attempt to develop a sharper definition of religious belief was surely premised on his own convictions about what constituted genuine religious faith. His procedure here is unavoidable. Any study of religious belief and religious people must be rooted in some decisions about what is to count as religious faith and what is not. Shall I count the man down the street who sells certificates of ordination out of his garage to help others evade income taxes? Shall I count the television evangelist who fleeces millions from the faithful, while living an extravagant and immoral life himself? If not, why not? I would argue that it is because we need to distinguish genuine religious faith from huckstering and con artistry, and that distinction is essentially an evaluative one.

An empiricist might respond to these arguments by conceding that some or all of the concepts I have discussed are value-laden, but arguing that this does not show that psychology must be value-laden. Perhaps what I have shown is simply that psychology should avoid these concepts and others which are like them.

I will admit that it is possible for psychology to attempt to do this, and to succeed to some degree. I have already said that not all concepts are equally value-laden, so it is possible for psychology to seek to employ those concepts which are less value-laden. Often this is not really a matter of avoiding all value commitments, but simply a matter of employing those concepts whose tacit value commitments are widely accepted. It is true, I think, that value judgments which are widely accepted are less likely to be noticed as value judgments. And I think that for certain types of research this procedure may be completely justified. I am certainly not claiming that psychologists must go out of their way to employ concepts whose application will be highly controversial.

However, I do not think psychology can avoid all value-laden concepts in all situations, and I do not think psychologists should even try to do this. The reason is that the price of abandoning value-laden concepts, or using only the most minimally loaded, least controversial concepts, is a lack of relevance. Personally, I am interested in friendship, aggression, obedience and authority, religion, and art. A psychology which has nothing to say about these subjects is a psychology which lacks relevance to some of our most significant concerns as human beings.

One might object at this point that the value element in the use of these concepts is neutralized so long as psychologists give explicit definitions and make no claim that their definitions match up with ordinary usage. Thus, psychologists can define "altruism" or "religion" any way they wish, so long as it is clear that this is a technical term in the study.

While I am all for explicit definitions and clear criteria for the use of concepts, I do not believe that this allows psychologists to escape taking responsibility for the value judgments embedded in their definitions. The problem is that so long as our ordinary terminology is employed, reports and interpretations of the study will inevitably be read as relevant to the real world. The psychologist may be studying "religion" in a technical sense, and not religion in the ordinary sense, but such a study will always be read as giving us information about religion in the ordinary sense, not just "religion." So it is not enough to explicitly define and give criteria for the concepts. Those definitions and criteria must be defended as reasonable, and this includes the value-dimensions of those concepts and criteria.

Do Facts Alone Determine Which Theories Should Be Held?

I have characterized the claim that psychology should be value-free as a twofold claim: that psychologists should use value-free concepts, and that psychologists should only allow facts to determine which theories are acceptable. In criticizing the first claim, I have been implicitly criticizing the second as well, since if values and facts cannot be sharply distinguished, and the concepts we use to describe the facts have value implications, then the claim that theories are accepted or rejected solely on the basis of facts is untenable.

Now it is important to be clear about what I am and am not claiming in arguing that values have a role to play in theory selection. The advocates of value-free science are rightly concerned at this point to safeguard crucial scientific values, particularly the commitments to honesty and truth. An essential element in science is a willingness to look honestly at evidence and not allow one's hopes and wishes to shape one's data. Unless we are willing to do this, there is no hope that data can actually correct erroneous views and support correct ones. Please do not read what follows as providing support for wish fulfillment, or as providing any justification for tampering with or falsifying data, or dealing dishonestly in any way with evidence.

What must be recognized is the naivete of the empiricist picture of theory selection as determined solely by the "facts." First, we must see that facts are always theory-laden and thus embody interpretive judgments. Facts are interpreted; they do not come bearing their own infallible rules for assessing their significance. Secondly, we must remember that theories hardly ever face the facts alone; they are incorporated in networks and systems. If a network of theories seems not to fit with some facts, a choice still must be made about which theory to modify, and the facts do not usually give a straightforward answer to the problem.

Even aside from these problems, the simple truth of the matter is that theories are always underdetermined by the facts. Take any cluster of points on a graph, and it will always be possible to draw indefinitely many lines to connect them or represent them.

How then do we choose from among all the theories which are compatible with the facts? Scientists choose on the basis of the values which they hold. They believe that true theories are likely to be simple, elegant, and to give rise to new discoveries and fruitful research. These criteria are by no means derived from the facts; they are essentially value criteria. Scientists are human beings, and human beings value simplicity, elegance, and intellectual fertility.

One more factor weighs heavily in theory selection. When faced with two rival theories, one of which is discordant with many of our other beliefs, while the other is consistent with those beliefs, we do not hesitate to choose the latter, even when the two are equally faithful to the facts. Scientific judgments presuppose what Michael Polanyi has called tacit knowledge, background beliefs of which we may not be fully cognizant.[4]

Suppose the following fact to be true: some gambler consistently "calls" the results of a particular football team. Two explanations are proffered. One is that the gambler's success is due to ESP; the other explanation is that a fix is on. Most of us would unhesitatingly prefer the second. We know that professional gamblers have often tried to fix the outcome of athletic events; such an explanation is highly consistent with what we know and believe about humans. We have, on the other hand, little reason to believe in ESP and no plausible theory concerning how such an ability could be exercised.

When we combine this picture of theory as underdetermined by data with this latter insight, we can see that there is room for values to play a role in theory selection, without making a case for wish fulfillment or data tampering. Two psychologists who are equally honest with the data can still interpret the results of an experiment in

4. Michael Polanyi, *The Tacit Dimension* (Garden City, N.Y.: Doubleday, 1966).

radically different ways. A classical example of this is the dispute over Wolfgang Köhler's famous experiments concerning insight. In one experiment Köhler placed a chimp in a cage with a banana hung out of reach. Three boxes were also placed in the cage. The banana was located high enough so that the chimp could reach it only by placing the three boxes on top of each other. After fruitlessly trying to reach the banana, the chimp pondered the situation, and then, with a clear expression which seemed to mean "I've got it," suddenly stacked the boxes and reached the banana.

To the Gestalt psychologists and to cognitivists today the experiment clearly suggests that the best explanation for the behavior is a process of thought culminating in a moment of insight. Radical behaviorists, however, refuse to accept this interpretation. Recently Robert Epstein, who was an associate of B. F. Skinner, has produced a film which allegedly reproduces the phenomenon with pigeons, and explains the apparent "insight" as the result of operant learning![5] Here it seems clear that the radical behaviorist's theoretical belief that all conscious processes can be reduced to overt behavior is the key factor in how the experiment is interpreted.

Frequently, I believe, the other beliefs which make a theory more or less plausible to us will include value beliefs. Let us take for an example a controversial area such as homosexual behavior. Some people believe that homosexual behavior is morally wrong; others view it as simply an alternative sexual preference or life-style. Suppose that a gay-rights group does research purporting to show that gay people are better adjusted and more emotionally healthy on average than other people. Someone who believes that homosexual behavior is morally wrong and a misuse of sexuality would rightly be suspicious of this research and reluctant to agree without careful scrutiny

5. Robert Epstein and B. F. Skinner, *Cognition, Creativity, and Behavior: The Columban Simulations* (Champaign, Ill.: Research Press, n.d.).

of the definitions employed, research methods used, and
so on. Even after careful scrutiny, such a person might
well reasonably conclude that further study is needed, pre-
ferring to reserve judgment. From the other side, a gay-
rights advocate might be equally suspicious of research
done by conservatives purporting to show that homosexual behavior is associated with neuroses.

Allport's studies of prejudice, discussed in the preceding
section, are an illustration of the same point. Allport's
own religious faith was surely one factor which led him
to be suspicious of the research which showed that religious faith is positively associated with prejudice. What
I wish to claim is that such an attitude can be reasonable,
and does not imply that someone is being dishonest or
failing to face the facts.

Of course if we are really open to the facts correcting
our theories, there are limits to how far we can go in
discounting research. Nevertheless, everyone does in fact
allow their general beliefs about the world to shape which
theories they see as plausible. There are many cases where
the evidence does not suffice to establish one theory decisively, and yet researchers (and ordinary human beings)
must, provisionally at least, decide what to believe. There
are also many decisions to be made concerning whether
a theory should be abandoned when there is some support
for the theory, but also some recalcitrant data. How tenaciously should a psychologist hold onto a theory in such
a case? Our general beliefs, including our value beliefs,
will certainly be one legitimate factor here, and there is
no reason why Christians should not allow their Christian
convictions to function in this context, if they are really
convinced that their beliefs are true.

Reasons and Rationalizations:
Evaluating the Other's Story

I have argued that value-free psychology is tied to a
morally objectionable divorce of reality and value which

leads to moral nihilism, and that psychologists do not have to divorce their work as scientists from values, both because the concepts psychology employs have value implications, and because, in cases where theory is underdetermined by data, value beliefs will be among the background beliefs psychologists will legitimately bring to bear in deciding which theories to accept or at least provisionally maintain. Besides these considerations, there is one further reason why value-critical psychology is legitimate. This reason has particular relevance with respect to humanistic and phenomenological psychologists.

Some humanistic psychologists would accept much of my argument so far. In particular, the claims of chapters 3 and 4 that psychology must be a psychology of meaning will be applauded. Furthermore, the humanistic psychologist might concede that the language of a psychology which takes meaning seriously will inevitably be value-charged. However, the humanist may still maintain that there is a sense in which the psychologist must strive for a value-neutral if not value-free stance.

The humanistic psychologist may agree with my claim in chapter 2 that an understanding of human behavior must be rooted in an understanding of the normative rules which shape that behavior, and that understanding such rules cannot be reduced to knowing empirical regularities. It follows from this that the descriptions of human behavior given by psychologists cannot be strictly value-free. Perhaps, however, the psychologist can still attain a stance of value-neutrality. Surely, the task is not to evaluate the rules which people follow, but merely to describe them, and to determine if they do indeed follow those rules.

There surely is a place in psychology for phenomenology, conceived as the attempt to understand the behavior of an individual or community as that individual or community would understand it. However, I do not believe that this enterprise could be the whole of psychology, at least not in a fallen world. The difficulty stems from the obvious fact that people are often unclear about what they are doing, and that they frequently deceive themselves about what they are doing. Psychologists who want to determine what people are really up to must inevitably ask about the adequacy of the self-understanding of the person or people they are studying, and there is no way to do this in a value-neutral way. The clinician who questions the distortions of reality of a severely depressed or psychotic client is a clear illustration of a procedure which is part and parcel of psychology generally.

Growing up in the South, I knew many sincere defenders of segregation. These people would hotly deny that segregation was a racist policy, and would have indignantly denied any sympathy with the more blatant racism of the Klan or the White Citizens Councils. They vigorously defended the principle of "separate but equal" as best for both races. I knew people who would give generously of their time and money for black Christian education, but would nevertheless refuse to allow blacks to join their own churches.

Any phenomenological, value-neutral description of these people would have totally falsified the nature of their behavior with respect to race. The fact is, there were massive contradictions between their professed love for people of another race and the suffering which the segregated policies they supported actually inflicted. To get at the truth, a value-critical perspective was essential, a perspective which did not rest content with merely understanding people's behavior as the people themselves understood it, but critically evaluated that self-understanding.

The phenomenon of self-deception, and its importance, should certainly be no news to Christians. Christians not only believe in the pervasiveness of sin in human life, but have traditionally recognized that one of the primary effects of sin is that the intellect of the sinner is clouded.

The effects of this clouding are especially significant with respect to gaining self-understanding.

One way of seeing the point here is to focus on the distinction between reasons and rationalizations. Meaningful behavior is behavior done for reasons, but to what degree are people aware of the true reasons for their actions? This is not an easy question, either in general or in particular cases. In particular cases there will be many factors to consider in deciding. But one factor will be an assessment of the adequacy of the reasons brought forward.

That the adequacy of a reason is one factor in deciding whether it really plays a role is clear in clinical contexts. Consider the case of a man who refuses to speak to his wife because, he says, she occasionally overcooks his eggs. The cruelty of his behavior and the pathetic unreasonableness of his justification show clearly that his self-understanding is askew. Even if we put aside the question of why he should not cook his own eggs, it simply is not reasonable to punish a person so severely for a minor mistake. Some game is being played here; there is anger and an attempt to dominate the other. If the man is aware of this game, he is a sadist; if he is not aware, then the reasons he gives for his behavior are not his real reasons.

This does not mean that behavior which is irrational cannot make sense to the agent. The self-deceived person often is sincere, at least to a degree. And there is merit in the project of understanding the world from the perspective of the agent, even when the project is carried to the extreme of an R. D. Laing,[6] who sees the beliefs of the schizophrenic as a reasonable response to an unlivable situation. (I think Laing is right about this in some cases.) And there is an important distinction to be made between the judgment that someone's reasons are bad reasons from an objective standpoint, and the judgment that the rea-

---

6. See R. D. Laing, *The Politics of Experience* (New York: Ballantine, 1967).

sons given by the person are not really reasons at all, but rationalizations which actually play no role in motivating the action. We must be careful to recognize the case of the person whose reasons are really reasons, and who is to be seen as worthy of respect, even admiration, even if we think that the person's reasons are mistaken.

Evaluation of the adequacy of a person's reasons is only one factor among many in distinguishing reasons from rationalizations. Equally important is empirical data showing a lack of congruence between the person's alleged principles and his behavior. Evaluation is a significant factor, nonetheless. One of the crucial tasks of psychology is to explore the nature and types of human self-deception. I do not think this task can be carried out in a value-neutral way. The humanist who wants to shirk this task is contributing to the pervasive value relativism and nihilism of our age, by refusing to make value judgments which he regards as defensible and subject to rational scrutiny. Here the relativism of humanistic psychology and the naturalism of empiricist psychology reveal an underlying affinity. Both ultimately see values as non-rational, subjective preferences, divorced from knowledge and reality. Christian psychology must be different.

6

Taking Freedom Seriously in Psychology

I began with the question of whether the ideal of Christian psychology was a coherent and viable one. The chief barrier to such an ideal is still, I claimed, the empiricist view of psychology which dominates the profession. I then argued that psychology as a scientific discipline has three faces: the empirical face, the interpretive face, and the value-critical face. Each is legitimate and each stands in need of the other. Since empirical research itself incorporates hermeneutical and value-critical elements, the empiricist is in no position to reject interpretive and value-critical activity as a legitimate part of psychology.

That psychology is interpretive in character implies that psychologists must strive to be wise as well as knowledgeable. To be a first-rate psychologist one must understand human life. Such an understanding is gained in the course of living, not just through academic study, and is intimately related to the character of the psychologist.

In chapter 5 I argued that a psychology which took

meaning seriously would also be a value-critical psychology, rather than a value-free or value-neutral endeavor. The wisdom which psychologists should pursue to attain their ends requires rejecting the modern divorce of facts from values, and recognizing that questions about the value of a thing cannot be completely separated from questions about its nature.

The acceptance of these claims would open the door to Christian psychology. The wisdom to be gained through Christian faith, both in theological and biblical learning and through Christian experience, should permeate the character of the Christian psychologist and shape the perspective from which she views human behavior. Christian convictions about the nature and purpose of human life, and the goodness and badness of kinds of actions, could explicitly influence the kinds of concepts used to describe human behavior, the ways in which those concepts are defined, and even the kinds of theories which are regarded as plausible. Interpretations of behavior and the meaning of actions would not necessarily be the same as those offered by non-Christian psychologists.

The argument so far has focused on what I would call the epistemological and ethical dimensions of Christian psychology. Nevertheless, implicit in this argument has been a particular metaphysic which is the other key element in Christian psychology.

In viewing human beings as meaning-seeking and valuing beings, I have implicitly rejected the claim that human behavior can generally be explained by the same principles which suffice to explain animal behavior, as well as the claim that psychology should model itself on the natural sciences. Though I would not underestimate the extent to which even animals can behave in meaningful ways (recent research into animal communication is certainly promising), no one would wish to suggest that a study of their behavior is generally dependent on understanding the beliefs of such animals about their behavior, still less that to properly understand what such animals are about, we must make critical value judgments about their meanings. Why not? The answer clearly is that there is something unique about human beings. They are persons. A Christian psychology takes account of this unique status.

This is not the place to articulate a full account of what it means to be a person.[1] A full account would focus on the following elements: consciousness; self-consciousness; social relatedness; capacity for action, reflection, and emotion; and in the case of human beings, being embodied and all that being a physical creature entails.

What I wish to do is to select one crucial characteristic of persons, which I believe would be highlighted in a truly Christian psychology, namely, the capacity for responsible, free action. I select this characteristic because it is crucial, it is linked to seeing human beings as meaning-seeking and valuing beings, and it is often thought to be especially troublesome for scientific psychology. What I hope to show is that a belief in robust, genuine freedom is not a problem but an asset to psychology.

The Significance of Freedom
for Christian Psychology

Behaviorists and Freudians agree that all human behavior is causally determined, even if they agree on nothing else. Even moderate and "cognitive" behaviorists are usually careful to claim that they are not denying that

1. I have attempted to offer such an account elsewhere. In addition to *Preserving the Person* (Downers Grove: Inter-Varsity, 1977), see "Healing Old Wounds and Recovering Old Insights: Towards a Christian View of the Person for Today," in *Christian Faith and Practice in the Modern World: Theology from an Evangelical Point of View*, ed. Mark Noll and David Wells (Grand Rapids: Eerdmans, 1988). See also "The Self in Contemporary Psychology," in *Psychology and the Christian Faith* (Grand Rapids: Baker, 1986).

there are lawful regularities which govern human behavior. The complexities of human activity may make it impossible to discover the underlying laws, but there is great confidence that such laws are present. In the face of this consensus, it is not surprising that Christian psychologists have not taken a clear stand in favor of freedom. Some have been tempted by determinism because of a theological emphasis on the sovereignty of God. Many have been content to assert that we must have our cake and eat it too; freedom and determinism represent an unsolvable paradox where both elements must be affirmed.

Yet there are strong elements in Christian faith which make it urgent to hold to a strong conviction that human beings are free, responsible beings. Even Calvinists such as Jonathan Edwards have insisted that the sovereignty of God must be understood in a way which is consistent with human freedom, though one may question whether Edwards's understanding of freedom is adequate.

The crucial reason for this is the importance of placing the responsibility for sin squarely on human beings. Hardly anyone wants to claim that God causally determines humans to sin and allows them no choice in the matter. To say otherwise is to go against some of our most central moral convictions. Christians see the God of the Bible as a God of justice, who holds people accountable for their deeds, and who therefore created humans as free creatures who can properly be held responsible.

Of course God is a God of love and mercy, and not only justice. But even God's mercy implies human freedom. God seeks a faithless people in self-sacrificing love, but he seeks them in such a manner as to allow them to spurn his overtures, even to that permanent choice to spurn him which constitutes hell. I will not attempt to argue here with those whose motivation for embracing determinism is theological. Rather I wish to speak to those who, like myself, believe that it is essential for Christians to affirm that human beings possess responsible freedom, but who see such a commitment as being in tension with the perspective of scientific psychology.

One tempting move for the Christian psychologist at this point is to opt for methodological determinism. The methodological determinist says that determinism is not the final or whole truth about human persons. It is simply a working assumption to be made when approaching human beings from the psychological perspective.

I used to believe that methodological determinism was a viable Christian view, but I no longer do. The temptation to move from methodological determinism to genuine metaphysical determinism is too strong. If determinism works as a hypothesis, why does it work? The most obvious answer is that it is because determinism is true. In that case the psychological perspective gives us the truth about human nature.

I wish to show that the Christian psychologist does not have to assume determinism, even as a working hypothesis. Determinism is not supported by any empirical findings of psychology, and it is not necessary to assume determinism in order to do psychological research.

I will show that contrary opinions are largely rooted in confusions. The confusions are popular, but they are still confusions. The chief confusions concern the nature of freedom and determinism, the nature of causation, and the nature of explanations of human activity.

The Nature of Determinism:
Hard and Soft

If freedom and determinism are clearly and properly defined, three positions on the issue can be distinguished.[2] Two of these positions are forms of determinism.

2. See William Hasker, *Metaphysics: Constructing a World-View* (Downers Grove: Inter-Varsity, 1983), chapter 2, for a lucid explanation of the possible positions.

A deterministic view of human behavior is one that claims that all human behavior has causes which make any other behavior than that which in fact occurs impossible. All determinists accept this claim, though they may disagree about the nature of the causes which are operative.

An important distinction must be made, however, between soft determinists and hard determinists. The difference between the two is not, as many think, that hard determinists say that all behavior is determined, while soft determinists say that only most of it is. Nor is the difference that soft determinists view causes as merely influencing, but not strictly determining, their effects. Since determinism is a universal thesis, the claim that some human behavior is not rigidly caused is not a form of determinism at all, but a denial of determinism.

The difference between hard and soft determinism is not that one is more deterministic than the other. The difference is a disagreement about the implications of determinism. The hard determinist believes that if determinism is true, then human freedom and responsibility do not exist. Since hard determinists believe that determinism is indeed true, they draw the conclusion that our convictions about human free will and moral responsibility are part of a mythology which must be discarded. Hard determinists, then, are incompatibilists. They claim that freedom and determinism cannot both be true.

Soft determinists, on the other hand, are compatibilists. They believe that it is possible in this case to have your cake and eat it too. Determinism is just as true for them as it is for hard determinists, but soft determinists believe that it is also true that human beings are sometimes free and responsible for their actions. There is no contradiction between viewing the same action as causally determined and yet free.

The soft determinist raises a challenge which must be faced. Before attempting to defend freedom against determinism, we must first decide whether it is necessary to choose between them. So the first question to be decided is whether compatibilism is true.

One well-known version of compatibilism has been espoused in Christian circles by Donald M. MacKay.[3] I will not treat MacKay's views here, partly because I have criticized them in print elsewhere, and partly because I think that MacKay's views reduce in the end to a version of the more standard type of compatibilism.

For the compatibilist, the crucial move in dissolving the dilemma of freedom and determinism is to define the terms very carefully. As the compatibilist sees it, true freedom is not lack of determination, but self-determination. Simply being determined does not mean lack of freedom; to lack freedom is rather to be determined by a certain type of cause, an external cause.

A simple illustration will help us to see what is meant. Suppose I am walking down the street of a major city, and I see someone soliciting funds for suffering victims of war in Central America. I am touched by the appeal and make a contribution. This is a free act, says the soft determinist, not because it is undetermined, but because it is caused by my own inner desires. (Or wishes or volitions; different forms of determinism propose different inner mental causes, but they all see free actions as caused by a person's inner mental states.) No one coerced me to make the donation; it is what I wanted to do.

It is true that my desire to make the donation is caused. Doubtless what psychologists call my "learning history" made me receptive to the appeal, or perhaps some natural biological urge to help my fellow human beings was operative. But the fact that the desire which led to the act was causally determined ultimately by my environment

3. For a good statement of Donald M. MacKay's views, see *Brains, Machines and Persons* (Grand Rapids: Eerdmans, 1986). For critiques of MacKay, see chapter 9 of my *Preserving the Person* and William Hasker, "MacKay on Being a Responsible Mechanism: Freedom in a Clockwork Universe," *Christian Scholar's Review* 8, no. 2 (1978), with a response by MacKay and counter by Hasker, pp. 130–52.

or genetic heritage is irrelevant, according to the soft determinist. The desire was mine, and I was free in this case to do what I wanted to do, and that is what freedom really is.

The situation would be very different if I had been accosted by a mugger who took my money after threatening my life. In this case I also give money, and again my act is causally determined. However, in this case I am acting against my own desires; I am caused to do what I do by an external power.

This compatibilist view that the opposite of freedom is not causal determination but external coercion is appealing, but I do not think it is ultimately acceptable. I do not believe that the kind of freedom the soft determinist defends is the kind which is necessary for moral responsibility. True moral responsibility requires us to be able to say to a person who has performed an act, "You had a choice; you could have done otherwise." But in the soft determinist view, there is a clear sense in which the choice could not have been any different. Given the causal background of the act, no other act was possible. And since the causes of my act were themselves caused, then no other act was really possible.

Soft determinists have one line of response here. They can argue that there is a sense in which a person who acts freely "could have done otherwise." I could have done something different with my money than make the donation to people in Central America *if I had wanted to.* Nothing prevented me from doing just what I wanted to do, and nothing would have prevented me from doing something different if I had wanted to do that.

However, the fact that I could have done something different if I had wanted to seems irrelevant to me, for the fact is that given my past history, I could not have wanted anything else. Furthermore, in the soft determinist view, given the fact that my wants are in place, my act was determined and no other act was possible. Saying that I could have done otherwise if I had wanted to is like saying that a corpse could get up and walk around if it were alive and healthy. The statement is true but not relevant, since such an action is not within the power of the corpse.

Suppose that a mad scientist attaches electrodes to your brain which can cause your desires to be activated by electrical signals he controls. This is not feasible today, and may never be, but it is the stock and trade of science fiction. The scientist controls your desires and volitions and gets you to act precisely as he wishes, but you are always able to do just what you want. Are you free in this situation? According to soft determinism you are, as long as you are able to do what you want to do.

If the soft determinist objects that in such a case your desires would no longer be your own, since they are controlled by the mad scientist, the question is, Why are they not? In the soft determinist view, all my inner wants and desires are ultimately the product of external factors, and this is not supposed to affect the freedom I have. If we replace the mad scientist with the slow, impersonal forces of evolution and environmental conditioning, is your freedom thereby increased? I do not think that the "freedom" which the soft determinist offers us is the freedom demanded for moral responsibility.[4] To be morally responsible, I must have a real choice to perform an action or not to perform an action, even if nothing about my past is different, unless my inability to do otherwise is due to previous free acts of mine.

The Nature of Freedom

I believe that many of the objections to accepting freedom stem from misconceptions about its nature. What does it mean to believe in free will?

4. For more rigorous philosophical defenses of this claim see Roderick Chisholm, "Freedom and Action," in *Freedom and Determinism*, ed. Keith Lehrer (New York: Random House, 1966), and Peter Van Inwagen, *An Essay on Free Will* (Oxford: Clarendon, 1983).

To distinguish belief in free will in the strong sense from the soft determinist kind of freedom, philosophers have coined the term *libertarianism.* (Libertarianism should not be confused with political libertarianism. A metaphysical libertarian can be a socialist politically.) Libertarians agree with hard determinists that compatibilism is false. They disagree with hard determinists, obviously, about the truth of determinism. Notice, however, that since determinism is a universal claim, the denial of determinism does not entail that all acts are free. Libertarianism is the claim that not all human actions are the inevitable product of past events. This leaves open the possibility that some human actions, perhaps even most human actions, are determined.

The libertarian believes that two types of causality are at work in the world, usually called event causality and agent causality. Event causation is the kind of causation which the natural sciences investigate, where one event or set of events leads to another event or occurrence. Agent causality is a causal chain in which the ultimate or "first cause" of the series of events is not another event, but a person, an agent.[5] If one thinks that event causation is the only kind of causation, there will be a strong tendency to think of human behavior in terms of this model. If one does this, then the causation which the self exerts will be understood as events occurring within the self (desires, volitions, or cognitive states) causing the person's actions, with those inner events themselves caused. In this model, the self is a place through which a causal stream flows.

The libertarian thinks that this is the wrong way to understand agent causality. In the libertarian view, agent causality is a basic type of causal power. Persons some-

5. The concept of agent causation is worked out by Roderick Chisholm, who initially called this form of causation "immanent causation." See "Freedom and Action." Perhaps the fullest classical development of this concept is found in Thomas Reid. See his *Essays on the Active Powers of the Human Mind* (Cambridge, Mass.: MIT Press, 1969).

times freely initiate actions without being determined to do so by any previous events occurring outside or inside the self.

Agent causality is admittedly mysterious from a third-person point of view. But what one should ask in this situation is whether agent causality is really any more mysterious than event causality. One can argue, in fact, that we really have a better grasp of agent causality, because our whole understanding of "cause" stems from our experience of ourselves as agents. When we act, we experience ourselves as creatures who can make a difference to the world.

In any case a Christian should not be afraid to affirm the coherence of the notion of agent causation, because this is the most basic type of causation for Christians. God is a person and the supreme cause of nature, with all its causal forces. God's creative activity is surely not to be understood as determined by events occurring within the divine mind, as if God were simply the inevitable product of some divine psychological laws. Since agent causality takes place when God creates and sustains the universe, why is it not possible when those creatures act whom God created in his own image to be responsible stewards over the rest of creation?

Scientific Objections to Libertarianism

I shall not attempt to respond to theological and philosophical objections to libertarianism. My concern is rather with the notion that libertarianism is a barrier to scientific psychology. It is commonly thought that libertarianism presumes that human actions are ahistorical, unpredictable, uncaused, and unexplainable, and these qualities would indeed be fatal ones for psychology if they really were implications of the libertarian view. I shall try to show that none of these follow from a libertarian view.

Does Libertarianism Imply That Human Actions Are Ahistorical?

One misconception of the libertarian view is that it sees human beings as ahistorical, completely uninfluenced by their past or by their environment, free to invent themselves anew at every moment. While this may be true of some extreme libertarians, such as the French existentialist Jean-Paul Sartre, it is by no means an implication of the position or a common view.

One can hold that human behavior is heavily influenced by the past without holding that the past always makes what a person does inevitable. People are always shaped by their past; many times a person's past leaves no real choice. All the libertarian maintains is that the past does not *always* make the outcome inevitable.

My past may severely limit my choices, and it may heavily weight my choices. Sometimes it may leave me no choice at all. But these heavy influences do not rule out freedom as a factor in my history. Sometimes, in fact, my lack of freedom may be traced to the misuse of freedom in my history. A drug addict may be unable to resist taking the drug today because of previous occasions in which he freely chose to take the drug. Real free choices have real consequences, and those consequences may include a loss or diminution of freedom for oneself and others. This is, incidentally, why libertarianism is fully compatible with a belief in original sin. To believe in original sin is to believe that we human beings have collectively so misused our freedom by rebelling against God that we are currently powerless to restore a relationship to God by our own efforts. Even the fact that we are slaves to sin points to our freedom; it simply underscores the fact that freedom is historical.

Does Libertarianism Imply That Human Behavior Is Unpredictable?

I have already argued, in chapter 2, that the discovery of regularities is an essential aspect of psychology, and that such empirical knowledge is essential to the interpretive and value-critical dimensions of psychology. If human behavior is basically unpredictable, then of course no such regularities can be found, and the empirical face of psychology will be blank. However, a libertarian does not need to claim that human behavior is generally unpredictable or that there are no regularities to be discovered.

First of all, even perfectly free actions may be regular and predictable, since free beings, if they are reasonable, will act consistently. This means that their behavior will be similar in similar circumstances (the circumstances including of course the cultural and historical context). Since people are not perfectly rational, genuine freedom means that regularities of behavior, which are not true natural laws, cannot be expected to be totally invariant. The actual regularities discovered by psychologists are, however, always probabilistic in character and culture-bound at least to some degree, and they allow for some variation.

The historical limitations on freedom discussed in the previous section are another reason why human behavior is predictable. The past history and present environment of a person strongly shape what options are possible and weight those options. This means that some responses are going to be far more probable than others in certain circumstances. This shows that human freedom is limited and historical, but does not show that it is not real.

Does Libertarianism Imply That Free Actions Are Uncaused?

The critic of libertarianism might concede that libertarianism can see human persons as historical beings, and even allow for some predictability in human behavior. However, the critic might insist, libertarianism still throws a monkey wrench into science by implying that free human actions have no cause in the ordinary scientific sense.

After all, says the critic, you yourself have insisted that

free actions, though they are not uncaused, must be seen as caused by the self. But to attribute an action to the work of the self, rather than seeing it as the outcome of a set of events, seems to make explanation of actions too easy and to eliminate the search for the kinds of causes scientists rightly concern themselves with. Since the explanation "He did it because he chose to" is always available, other explanations are unnecessary. And an explanation like this one, which explains every action, is scientifically useless.

To answer this objection, I must say a little more about the notion of a cause. In philosophy the term *cause* is often used to refer to a set of conditions which is sufficient to bring about a particular outcome. If that is what is meant by "cause," the libertarian will insist that free actions are uncaused, since there is no set of events, independent of the free choice brought about by the agent himself, which is sufficient to bring about the act in a case of free action. Otherwise the act would not be free.

However, this is not the only sense of "cause." Both in ordinary experience and in psychology the term is often used in a looser way to refer to a condition which is necessary to an outcome, but not sufficient, or even to refer to a condition which makes an outcome probable but does not guarantee it. As an illustration, take the case of a young person who has had an accident while under the influence of alcohol. What is the cause of the young person's decision to drink and drive? One might point to the easy availability of alcohol in the young person's high school and the social acceptability of teenage drinking. Someone else might point to the fact that the young person had no sense of purpose and meaning in his life; perhaps he was drinking to dull an ache. Somebody else might point out that the young man had very low self-esteem and had harsh, rejecting parents. Someone might point to a failure on the part of teachers or other responsible adults to heed various warning signs. And still another theorist might point to the addictive properties of alcohol itself and the physiological vulnerability of the young person to addiction.

In a particular case all of these factors may play a role. Each might be necessary in the sense that if one factor had been different the tragedy would not have occurred, yet no one of them, nor even all of them together, may be sufficient. Still other factors may have played a role, and one of these other factors may well have been a free choice on the part of the individual, either on the occasion of the accident or on some previous occasion.

If a cause is a condition which contributes to an event, including, in particular, necessary conditions, then all of these factors may be causes. If that is what we mean by "cause," then a belief in free choice in no way precludes a search for causes. Of course we have noted that a libertarian does not believe that all human behavior is free, but even where we believe genuine freedom is at work, it is always legitimate to look for other causes. The individual's free choice is one factor; there may be many forces at work which make it more likely that the individual will choose one way rather than another. So the libertarian by no means limits psychologists to choice as the sole cause of behavior.

In reality, the only types of causes psychologists ever discover anyway are necessary but not sufficient conditions or conditions which predispose but do not necessitate. They may find that child abusers are more likely to have been abused as children, and conclude that being abused is one cause of becoming an abuser. But there are plenty of people abused as children, probably an overwhelming majority, who themselves never become child abusers. So this factor is never more than one factor among many, another force to be considered as part of the total situation. All the libertarian wants to insist on is that freedom be viewed as a possible aspect of that total situation.

Does Libertarianism Imply That Free Actions Cannot Be Explained?

Another worry that psychologists have about allowing freedom into their bailiwick is that freedom shortcuts the search for explanations of human behavior. To say that a person performed an act because she chose to seems too easy, and it seems to preclude any scientifically verifiable explanation.

Our previous discussion about causation should alleviate this fear to a great extent. Once we realize that free actions can have causes (contributing conditions) in addition to the free choice of the agent, then it is obvious that such actions can also have other explanations than "she chose to do it." It will be true that the explanations in terms of external causes will be incomplete in the case of genuinely free actions, but incomplete explanations may still be useful. Almost all the explanations scientists actually give are in fact incomplete.

However, there is more to be said about the notion of explanation. Many psychologists use the term *reason* synonymously with "cause." Thus, to ask about a person's reasons for an action is to ask about the causes of the action. This is dangerous, because reasons are not causes in the ordinary scientific sense of the term. While I agree that some reasons are causes, not all of them are, and not all causes are reasons. A reason, when it is a cause, is a special type of cause.

Many psychologists are inclined to accept a particular model of explanation called the covering law model of explanation. According to this model, which owes its origins to the philosophy of logical positivism, explanation always requires a generalization, something which is at least similar to a law of nature. If we know that water always freezes at 32 degrees Fahrenheit, and we know there is water around and the temperature is 31 degrees Fahrenheit, we know that the water will freeze. If someone asks why, we have a ready explanation. The water will freeze because water always freezes under particular conditions, and the particular conditions are met. In this view explanation and prediction are very similar. The same information prior to an event allows you to make a prediction; after the event it allows you to make an explanation.

Though it needs refinement, the covering law model is a powerful and attractive one for events in the natural world and for some human behavior. However, it is not the only possible model for explaining human behavior, and it is not the model which is commonly relied upon in ordinary experience when people cite reasons for their behavior or the behavior of others. Many explanations of psychologists do not rely on the covering law model either, though this is not always noticed.

Let us take the case of a bank teller in need of money to finance an operation for his mother.[6] He figures out a way to embezzle a little money each day and alter the books to make it unlikely that he will be caught (so he thinks). If we ask what the reason for the teller's behavior is, an answer is near at hand. He needs the money urgently, reasons that he is unlikely to get caught, and (let us suppose) believes that his actions will not really hurt anyone: the bank's depositors are insured, and the owners of the bank are wealthy and will not miss a little extra profit.

The reason given is perfectly plausible and understandable. But notice that the explanation given nowhere cites anything like a law of nature or even a plausible generalization. It is not true that bank tellers are likely to embezzle money if they can; it is not even true that bank tellers who need money urgently are likely to do so. Even if we try to restrict the generalization to the teller in question, it is impossible to find one which is necessary to

6. This example is developed from one in Lessnoff.

the story. The teller may never have stolen anything in his life, so it is not necessarily true that he always or even usually does such things when he has the chance or when the circumstances permit. There may be some generalizations which apply to the case, but the point is this: we do not know any and do not need to know any to explain the behavior of the teller.

Why does the explanation work? It works because it cites a reason for the action. A reason is characteristically a set of desires and beliefs on the part of the agent. Given that the teller needs and wants money, believes he can get it this way, and believes that there is nothing wrong with the action, he has a reason for performing the action, a reason which at least to him looks like a good reason. The connection between a reason and an action is not merely contingent and external, as is the case for causes in nature, where the explanation does depend on a law of nature. There is no reason (that we know) why gravity should operate to obtain the effects it does; that is just the way it operates. A reason, on the other hand, establishes an intelligible connection between a certain action and the goals and beliefs of an agent. If you have been looking for a certain book for a year, strongly want it, find it in a bookstore, have the money to pay for it, and have no reason not to buy it, it makes sense that you will buy it. Given the agent's rationality, and that he has no powerful reasons to overrule his reason, we require no further explanation of a reasonable action. In particular, we do not need to know that other people would behave in a similar manner in other circumstances. If other people do not behave in such a manner, that means they are irrational, and that may call for an explanation, but it does not undermine the explanation of the rational action we normally accept.

I have taken some time to elaborate on the nature of a reason because I believe that psychologists frequently spend a great deal of time exploring and learning about the reasons people have for acting as they do. Their research shows that people are not always rational, and that the reasons people believe they have for doing something are not always the real reasons. But it is important to realize that a search for reasons is not necessarily a search for "covering" laws, or even lawlike generalizations.

The absence of covering laws is important, because one mark of a genuinely determined natural object, such as the objects in the solar system, is that their behavior is describable by such laws. In looking for reasons, therefore, psychologists are not necessarily looking for determining causes. A reason seems, in fact, to be the kind of cause which fits nicely into the libertarian picture of human action.

We have already seen that, in the libertarian view, free actions can be caused. Reasons seem to be just the sort of causes which could be part of the story of a free action without being the whole story. They contribute, in some cases decisively, without determining. This fits well with our ordinary experience. When asked if we had reasons for an action, we normally would say that we did, but we hardly think of those reasons as making the action unfree. Did I have reasons for agreeing to write this book? Of course. Was my act unfree because I had those reasons? Of course not. I had good reasons for agreeing to do the book, but I do not believe those reasons made the decision inevitable, or precluded any free choice.

Hermeneutics and Freedom

We can now see the epistemology and metaphysics of Christian psychology fit together. At the beginning of this chapter, I pointed out that the hermeneutical and value-critical character of psychology implies that there is a real difference between psychology and the other human sciences and those sciences which study impersonal nature. We can now see the ground of this difference more clearly.

Persons are free, responsible agents, and their behavior is not explained solely by laws of nature, but at least in part by reasons. The sufficiency of a reason to explain an action is intrinsically linked to the meaning of the reason, since it is the intelligible connection between a reason and an action that makes it possible for the reason to function as an explanation.

Human beings often act in regular, predictable ways, and knowledge of these regularities is valuable. However, these regularities must not be viewed as approximations to laws of nature; they are simply regularities. A knowledge of such regularities may help us to decide when freedom is really at work, and they may help us, as I argued in chapter 2, to determine when a reason is a genuine cause and not merely a rationalization. But the overall project of explaining human behavior more closely resembles history than natural science.[7] To explain what a person is doing is to give a narrative. The story will include many causal factors other than the person's free choice, but the ultimate goal is to tell a true story. To tell such a story one must understand both the actions and the context of the story, and see how they fit together in a coherent manner. A free being is a being whose life must be understood as a story, not as a set of instances of laws of nature.

Christian Psychology and Basic Assumptions

Is a psychology which takes meaning, values, and freedom seriously uniquely Christian? Certainly not. Many of the arguments I have given are echoed by such secular thinkers as Kenneth J. Gergen. What I would wish to maintain is that a psychology which takes meaning, val-

7. This conception of psychology is developed in detail in Donald E. Polkinghorne, *Narrative Knowing and the Human Sciences* (Ithaca, N.Y.: SUNY Press, 1988).

ues, and freedom seriously can be a distinctively Christian psychology, where Christian convictions make a difference to the way meanings, values, and freedom are understood.

I do think that Christians ought to be more receptive to these themes than secular thinkers because the picture of human personhood which is presupposed by such a psychology seems close to the picture which Christians assume to be true. Christians know that human beings are meaning-seeking creatures, that value considerations are intrinsic to their being, and that facts and values are not ultimately divorced. They know that human beings are free, responsible beings. The fact that other people can recognize these insights is a reflection of common grace, but it does not mean that these are not Christian insights.

Christians should have an easier time than non-Christians recognizing the possibility of agent causality and the causal efficacy of personal beliefs, desires, and volitions, since we believe that the ultimate cause of everything is not an event but a person. But if others see the same truths, that is to be welcomed, not feared.

One strength of a Christian psychology which takes these themes seriously is that there are built-in safeguards against the relativism and self-deification which plague secular thinkers who make similar anti-empiricist arguments.[8] In viewing the goal of psychological understanding as a narrative, Christians do not thereby give up the idea of truth and falsity because Christians believe that there is a true story for everyone's life. It is the story as God knows it. This story may be complex, and our human versions may never be more than approximations. But that is a consequence of our finitude, which plagues all human efforts to know. There is no reason to doubt that there is a true story to be known.

Christians also know that we are not the authors of our

8. For an illustration of the relativism which plagues parallel secular perspectives see Kenneth J. Gergen, *Towards Transformation in Social Knowledge* (New York: Springer-Verlag, 1982).

own stories. Our freedom is a limited, finite freedom, since we are creatures, and so the story will recognize how much of our lives is not of our own making. There is no reason to slight or ignore causal factors, both those which can be understood in terms of event causality, and the causal influences which can be traced to the actions of other agents. Human beings are like characters in a play who have the dignity of deciding some things about how their roles should be acted. But their decisions must be seen in the context of the limitations placed on them by the play itself and by their physical setting. And Christians know that the good actor is one who can creatively embody the intentions of the play's author.

7

Christian Psychology: *The Impossible Dream?*

In laying out the case for a psychology which takes meaning, values, and freedom seriously, I am simultaneously laying out a case for a psychology which could be distinctively Christian, informed by basic Christian convictions. In taking meaning seriously, such a psychology could do justice to the fact that human beings are spiritual creatures who do not live by bread alone, whose lives are constituted by meanings. In taking values seriously, such a psychology could do justice to the fact that not all meanings are created equal, and that human spirituality can be in harmony with its created structure or alienated from that structure. In taking freedom seriously, such a psychology could do justice to the fact that human beings are responsible for their spiritual condition, since they are created by God as responsible agents.

The difficulty of such an ideal should not be underestimated. It would require psychologists who are generalists as well as specialists, who seek wisdom as well as knowledge, who reject the assumption that all problems

131

can be solved by the right techniques, and who are interested in more than psychology. But, as the poets say, all things noble are as difficult as they are rare.

More troubling to me than the difficulty of carrying out the ideal is the suspicion that many Christian psychologists would rather not try. Despite my argument that a legitimate psychology would take meaning, values, and freedom seriously, and the evident ways that such a psychology would open doors to distinctively Christian approaches, I fear that old misconceptions still block many from considering such a quest. Let me try to remove some of these misconceptions with some final comments about the nature of Christian psychology.

The Nature of Christian Psychology

I would define Christian psychology as psychology which is done to further the kingdom of God, carried out by citizens of that kingdom whose character and convictions reflect their citizenship in that kingdom, and whose work as psychologists is informed and illuminated by Christian character, convictions, and understanding. What I have tried to do in this book is to sketch a conception of psychology which makes room for a Christian's personal character, beliefs, and goals to substantively shape the way psychology gets done. Careful thought about such an ideal can clear away many false ideas that are commonly thought to attach to the project.

For example, many object to the idea of Christian psychology on the grounds that the work of Christians in psychology is not unique. Of course one reason for this may be that Christians may not be doing truly Christian psychology. But even if Christians are working authentically as Christian scholars, it is true, as the critics suspect, that in many cases Christian psychologists will hold the same theories as non-Christians. The implicit assumption is that Christian psychology must be unique to be authentically Christian.

But why should we accept this assumption? Large segments of biblical morality are shared by Islamic moralists, Confucian moralists, and even secular moralists. Yet no one would, I hope, deny that there is such a thing as Christian ethics. If my ethical position is one which I hold as a Christian because I am a Christian, then it does not become non-Christian just because someone else may hold to a similar view.

The same thing is true for the Christian scholar generally, including the Christian psychologist. If a psychologist who is a Christian is thinking and working in a Christian manner about and with human beings, I am willing to call the product Christian psychology, whether it is utterly unique or similar to other views. In reality, of course, we would expect Christian psychologists to agree with their non-Christian colleagues at some points and disagree at other points. What makes their work Christian is its motivation and congruence with Christian attitudes and beliefs.

A second fear that some have about Christian psychology is that such an enterprise would be monolithic. No scholar would welcome the development of a "party line" to which he or she must adhere. I see no reason to think this would happen. If we look at disciplines like theology, ethics, and philosophy, where there are communities of scholars who are willing to identify what they do as scholars as Christian, we do not see uniformity, but a healthy pluralism and vigorous debate. Obviously, Christian psychologists will defend the idea of pluralism for the discipline of psychology, since Christian psychology implies that it is legitimate at least to try to develop Marxist psychology, feminist psychology, and other approaches to psychology. But Christian psychologists will defend the idea of pluralism within the project of Christian psychology as well, since Christians must recognize and respect differences in interpretation and understanding, and deal with those differences in love.

A third problem psychologists may have with the ideal of Christian psychology is that they fear it would lead to a ghetto for Christian psychologists. Such a ghetto is a real danger, but it can be avoided if two things are done.

First, Christian psychologists must continue to work within secular professional organizations and look for opportunities to demonstrate their competence and quality. This will mean that much work will have to be done in areas which are not "glamor" areas, and which are not especially crucial to Christian concerns. It is important to continue to show, as the Thomistic approach has done, that the Christian can be a good physiological psychologist, statistician, and so on.

Secondly, in communicating the results of distinctively Christian work, the audience must be kept in mind. If Christian psychology is good psychology, it will lead to new insights and fruitful research which may be recognizable as such by those who do not share the basic assumptions, just as operant conditioning theory led to (some) research which was recognizable as good by those who did not share B. F. Skinner's naturalistic assumptions. There is therefore the possibility of some common ground, since Christians and non-Christians live in God's world with the pressure of God's reality. To indicate such common ground, the Christian may, in presenting her findings, highlight evidence or reasons which would not seem so important in a Christian context. The Christian and the non-Christian may find themselves in some cases believing the same things for different reasons.

The situation is similar to that of the biblical ethicist, who holds a view because it is taught in Scripture, but argues for it on different grounds in a pluralistic democracy where public policy is being set. Such arguments can be valuable, even apologetically, since it is satisfying to see that biblical truth is confirmed by other evidence. In

a similar way, a Christian psychology which leads to fruitful insights and research lends plausibility to a Christian
world view generally. In saying this, I do not mean to
overestimate the common ground which may actually be
found, and I certainly think that Christians must be prepared, in this arena as in others, to suffer persecution for
their faith. But they should not seek persecution.

Thus, many common objections to the ideal of Christian
psychology do not stand up to critical scrutiny. There is,
however, one further objection that I have not addressed
which is the most serious of all.

Christian Psychology: Science or Ideology?

In talking about Christian psychology I have continued
to talk of psychology as a science. I fear that many will
find this ill-advised, including both friends and foes of the
enterprise. For in speaking of the legitimacy of values in
psychology, in legitimating Christian psychology but also
Marxist psychology and other such enterprises, what is
left of science? Have I not converted science into ideology?

I do not wish to abandon the word *science*. It is a word
with good historical roots in the Latin *scientia,* meaning
"knowledge." Fundamentally, I regard as scientific any reliable set of methods which a community of truth-seekers
employs to reach knowledge about the natural world. Implicit in the idea of such a community is the notion of
critical checks, in which claims made are seen as cor-
rectable. So we have two aspects of science, one positive
and one negative. Positively, science must make knowledge possible, or at least progress toward knowledge. Neg-
atively, scientific claims must be revisable, open to
challenge. Obviously, I have rejected the common understanding of science as requiring a single, supposedly neutral method for achieving these goals. What I must do to

show that Christian psychology can be science is to show that it can fulfill these two goals.

It might appear that the negative aspect of allowing one's beliefs to be open to revision would be the harder of the two for Christian psychology to fulfill, since connecting psychology to religious faith might appear to some to link it to dogmatism, but I do not think this is so. Scientific openness to revision of one's beliefs must be distinguished from actual doubt of a belief. Scientists may have the utmost confidence in their theories while remaining fully scientific in their attitudes. Conversely, the confidence Christian believers have in their faith need not be dogmatism; faith is willing to look honestly at problems and objections.[1] Of course I do not mean to suggest that Christian psychologists would have the same degree of confidence in their psychological theories that they have in their basic Christian beliefs. One may rightly have more confidence in one's faith than in one's reasoning concerning the implications of that faith for such other areas as scholarship.

So I think that the more difficult task for Christian psychology is not to show its openness to criticism, but to show that it is possible to reach knowledge in which a community of truth-seekers achieves substantial agreement. To show that this is possible would require me to do no less than produce Christian psychology, a task far beyond my ability or the ability of any single individual, since the only convincing proof that knowledge of a certain type is possible is to produce that knowledge. The best I can do toward showing that such knowledge is possible is to look at some analogous cases and defend the claim that knowledge is possible there.

If we think that genuine knowledge requires universal

---

1. See C. Stephen Evans, *Philosophy of Religion: Thinking About Faith* (Downers Grove: Inter-Varsity, 1985), pp. 159–79, for a fuller account of religious knowledge in this vein.

agreement, or agreement by all who investigate an affair, then it is obvious that Christian' psychology cannot lead to knowledge. But why should knowledge require universal agreement? The writer of John's Gospel tells us that he has written what he has written in order that those who read may know that Jesus is the Christ, the Son of God. Such knowledge is not gained by everyone who reads, but this does not mean the knowledge of those who do know is defective.

Lack of confidence that Christian psychology could lead to genuine knowledge seems tantamount to me to lack of confidence that Christianity itself can be known to be true. If Christianity is true, and can be known to be true, why should not those who study human beings as Christians gain true insights?

The psychologist who doubts that Christian psychology could lead to knowledge perhaps fears that psychology will be reduced to the status of philosophy, theology, or ethics, with their never-ending controversies. Leaving aside for a moment the question of whether psychologists do not have equally never-ending controversies, even with their supposed neutral scientific method, I would like to view the comparison of psychology with these fields in a more positive light. Though I know that we are finite, sinful beings, and that we cannot claim omniscience or infallibility, I would like to argue that knowledge can be gained in these fields. There are ethical truths, philosophical truths, and theological truths that I believe I know. Nor is this knowledge unique to me; it is widely shared in Christian communities. I believe that I know it to be true that the morally right action is not always the one which leads to the greatest pleasure and least pain for those affected. I believe that I know it to be true that a human person, though embodied, is not simply identical with his or her present physical body. I believe that I know that there is a God who made heaven and earth, who

called Abram out of Ur, and who is the God and Father
of our Lord Jesus Christ.

So even if Christian psychology means that psychology
will be more like philosophy and theology than is pres-
ently the case, that does not mean it cannot be science in
my sense, unless we are prepared to admit that no philosophical or theological knowledge is possible. And though
I think many Christian scholars are unconsciously tempted
to make such a denial, it seems to me to be a fundamental
failure of nerve which must be avoided.

Hermeneutics and the
Limits of Technique

We are dealing with fundamental philosophical issues
which have had a decisive impact on Western culture. One
way of developing the issue is to look at the area of hermeneutics, since I have explicitly argued that Christian
psychology will be a hermeneutical enterprise in part.

Many people believe that a lack of objectivity and rationality is inherent in such hermeneutical enterprises.
That is certainly part of the motivation for suppressing
and minimizing the hermeneutical aspect of psychology,
which I detailed in chapters 3 and 4. What about the
whole business of giving interpretations? Can interpretations be known to be right?

The area of hermeneutics is no longer, of course, limited
to biblical studies. Under the influence of Hans-Georg
Gadamer and other European philosophers, hermeneutics
has become a central area for philosophical reflection.[2] In
what follows, I shall try, in a very simplified and brief
manner, to say how I view the central issue.

Two opposing positions on the question of what consti-

2. See Richard Palmer, *Hermeneutics: Interpretation Theory in Schleier-
macher, Dilthey, Heidegger, and Gadamer* (Evanston, Ill.: Northwestern University Press, 1969), for an excellent introduction.

tutes a sound hermeneutic can be distinguished. On the one side are the proponents of seeing meaning as "authorial intent." According to this view the meaning of a text is essentially identical with the intentions of the author of the text. Those intentions can often be read from the text itself, so this view does not necessarily mean that one must have knowledge about the author. Still, when such knowledge is available, it is strong evidence for the correctness of an interpretation. In this view there is an objective standard for the correctness of an interpretation, and the ideal is a scientific method which will allow one to recapture this objective meaning. One can see this position in the "historical-critical" method in biblical studies and in jurisprudence in the doctrine of "original intent" which Edwin Meese and others have urged on the Supreme Court.

At the other extreme are the deconstructionists, followers of Jacques Derrida, who loudly proclaim the death of the author and of all "author-ity."[3] In this view every text in some way "subverts" itself and is fair game for the task of deconstruction. We deconstruct a text by breaking the hold of traditional and oppressive readings of the text, playing with the text, to create a meaning suitable for ourselves and our own times.

Neither of these positions seems credible to me without modification. The deconstructionist divorce of meaning and author seems too complete, and the rejection of authority seems to lead straight to relativism. The notion of true interpretation no longer makes sense in such a view.

The position favoring authorial intent is stronger, but still suffers grave difficulties. The primary one, it seems to me, is that even if we tie meaning to authorial intent, this still does not mean that the meaning becomes a completely fixed, totally objective entity. An author who writes

3. For a good illustration of this tendency see Mark Taylor, *De-Constructing Theology* (Chico, Calif.: Scholars Press, 1982).

something uses words which have meaning prior to his
using those words; the meanings are not invented by the
author and have a certain power which is independent of
the author. There are ambiguities in every text, and there
is what one might call a surplus of meaning, which gives
a text the power to surprise and educate its author. I myself have often felt that I have learned new things from
what I have written, and I have seen things in my texts
that I did not see at the time of writing. Principles enun-
ciated have implications which may not have been noticed
at the time; new situations may give a text new power to
speak in new ways. Thus it may not be possible to give an
interpretation of a text which is final. We can see this in
biblical texts, which need to be read and reread by every
generation, and from which new insights always seem to
be possible. The idea of progressive revelation in fact implies that God sometimes inspired the biblical authors to
say things whose full meaning could only be discerned
later, in the light of God's fuller revelation.

My conviction is that this characteristic of texts tolls
the death knell for any view of interpretation which implies that meaning can be determined through some technique which is guaranteed to produce the correct answer
if followed mechanically. Interpreting the meaning of a
text requires wisdom, discernment, and a certain imaginative understanding, as well as objective knowledge about
the situation and the culture. However, even here it is not
the case that anything goes.

Even if we recognize that the meaning of a text is not
a totally fixed entity, so that a plurality of interpretations
can be valid and legitimate, this is far from accepting the
claim that the text is totally plastic. Some readings do
make more sense than others. Christians who want to
stake their faith in biblical authority must accept this, but
it is a view which is also confirmed by experience. One
may wonder whether the central theme of Romans is justification by faith or the place of the Jewish people in the

history of salvation, but no one can reasonably argue that the major thrust of the letter is to teach a doctrine of infralapsarianism.

The fear which lurks here, and it is an old philosophical anxiety, is that if we abandon the claim that we have a technique which guarantees that we will arrive at the right result, then we will be left with epistemological anarchy. It is the same fear which underlies the tendency of psychologists to ignore hermeneutical questions. We must face the fact that we have no such techniques, in psychology or in biblical interpretation, no method which can be mechanically followed and is guaranteed to pulverize one's critics and silence all dissent. But our lack of such a technique does not mean that wise, truth-seeking people cannot arrive at truth and have good reasons for what they think true.

The example of hermeneutics is not merely an analogy if my view of psychology is correct. Discovering the truth about human behavior will be a matter of reading and interpreting a text, in this case the text of human activity. If we are confident that the hermeneutical problems can be solved in a field like biblical studies, I see no reason to think that it is impossible to make progress in understanding human behavior. Blinding ourselves to the hermeneutical aspects of psychology, and sticking tightly to those aspects of psychology which lend themselves to technique, is a good way of avoiding a certain type of anxiety, but it is not a good way to make progress in the field.

Good interpretations are those which are faithful to the facts, coherent, and illuminating. A good interpretation does not twist or distort the text, but reveals new dimensions of the text, patterns which would otherwise be overlooked. An interpretation shows its power by comparison with rival interpretations. If an interpretation can account for the insights of its rivals, and suggest insights which its rivals cannot make sense of, it is so far confirmed.

It is this process of engaging rival views in critical

dialogue which allows an interpretation to escape the relativistic self-enclosure which seems to haunt the hermeneutic circle. Critical dialogue with rivals—genuinely honest give-and-take, a willingness to learn and admit mistakes, an attempt to see the world through one's opponent's eyes—is the mark of a genuine science which is more than mere ideology. For this reason it is crucial that Christian psychology not take place in a ghetto. Christians must remain in the rough-and-tumble and give-and-take of the wider world. For this to be successful, that wider world will itself have to recognize the necessarily pluralistic character of psychology and the limits of technique in establishing assured, once-and-for-all results. Perhaps one way Christians can be salt in that wider world is by working for such a pluralistic environment.

A Future and a Hope

I conclude with a final word of hope and challenge. I know from talking with Christian psychologists that many are discouraged about the prospects of any meaningful change within the profession, and particularly pessimistic that such a secularized field will be open to anything that resembles Christian psychology.

Of course with God all things are possible, so the believer is never without hope in any kingdom endeavor. But I would like to recount some of the recent history of my own field, which may serve as inspiration that genuine change is possible. In the fifties and sixties, the prospects for Christian philosophy seemed as bleak as the prospects for Christian psychology. The number of Christian philosophers seemed very small, and almost none seemed to have much prominence. That situation has changed dramatically. New Christian philosophers have emerged and won genuine respect from their secular colleagues. Older, established philosophers have come out of the closet and revealed their Christian convictions. Others, equally prominent, have publicly converted to Christian faith. Most exciting of all, Christian philosophers have come together and formed a genuinely ecumenical community: talking together at conferences, publishing together, starting a recognized scholarly journal, all under the auspices of the Society of Christian Philosophers, with more than eight hundred members, several of whom are recent presidents of the American Philosophical Association. To me it seems true that with God all things are possible; if the spirit of God can move in philosophy, then can psychology be far behind?

To discover such possibilities, psychologists must be willing to take some risks. There is no question that publicly identifying oneself as a Christian psychologist implies the risk of losing professional esteem and status. However, it has always been the mark of authentic Christianity that true disciples have been willing to endure persecution for the cause of Christ. Though needless offense should of course be avoided, one mark of Christians is that they are willing to identify with a Jesus who told his disciples, "If the world hates you, keep in mind that it hated me first. If you belonged to the world, it would love you as its own. As it is, you do not belong to the world, but I have chosen you out of the world. That is why the world hates you" (John 15:18–19 NIV).

It is easy for the Christian academic to forget that the academic establishments are still, for the most part, "of the world." As disciples, we are called upon to be in the world but not of the world. Christian psychologists must think of themselves not merely as the Christians in the world of psychology, but as the psychologists of that community called the church, which always deserves their first loyalty. This community is in the world, and it may through God's grace have a positive impact on that world, including the world of academia. Such success cannot be counted upon, but ultimately this does not matter very much. The Christian is called, not to worldly success, but to faithfulness.

Suggestions for Additional Reading

General

Histories of Psychology

Those whose exposure to the history of psychology is limited to the "scientific" perspective of historians in the tradition of Edwin G. Boring's *A History of Experimental Psychology* (1929; 2d ed., New York: Appleton-Century-Crofts, 1950) can modify this perspective by consulting the following philosophically-oriented histories:

Max Dessoir, *Outlines of the History of Psychology*, translated by Donald Fisher (New York: Macmillan, 1912). Dessoir, a German psychologist, strongly emphasizes the soul.

George Sydney Brett, *A History of Psychology*, 3 vols. Vol. 1, *Ancient and Patristic*; vol. 2, *Mediaeval and Early Modern Period*; vol. 3, *Modern Psychology* (London: Allen and Unwin, 1912–1921). This classic is readily available in paperback in the edition edited and abridged by Richard Stanley Peters (London: Allen and Unwin, 1953).

Henryk Misiak, *The Philosophical Roots of Scientific Psychology* (New York: Fordham University Press, 1961). One of the earliest recent histories with a philosophical emphasis.

Richard Müller-Freienfels, *The Evolution of Modern Psychology*, translated by W. Béran Wolfe (New Haven: Yale University Press, 1935). Müller-Freienfels includes an excellent section on "the psychology with 'soul.' "

Abraham Aaron Roback, *History of American Psychology* (New

145

York: Library Publishers, 1952). Although Roback reveals a strong antireligious bias, this history is thorough in its coverage of both Protestant and Catholic philosophical psychologies.

Jay Wharton Fay, *American Psychology before William James* (New Brunswick, N.J.: Rutgers University Press, 1939). Fay explores the Calvinist theology and scholastic Platonism of the philosophers and theologians contributing to the tradition of moral philosophy, which was the major arena for the teaching of psychology prior to the advent of the experimental tradition.

Jacob Robert Kantor, *The Scientific Evolution of Psychology*, 2 vols. (Chicago: Principia, 1963). This history provides a broad philosophical background, despite the explicit bias of the author, who "began his historical studies with the conviction that the evolution of scientific psychology should be treated without the thralldom of transcendental assumptions and has found no basis for altering his opinion."

Robert Irving Watson, *The Great Psychologists: From Aristotle to Freud* (Philadelphia: Lippincott, 1963). Watson, a respected historian of psychology, provides a highly readable overview of historical philosophers and theologians. The latest edition of this text is available in paperback.

Sigmund Koch and David Leary, eds., *A Century of Psychology as Science* (New York: McGraw-Hill, 1985). This volume, which received the Association of American Publishers' Award, documents the recent revolution in historiography which is increasingly evident among members of Division 26 of the American Psychological Association, The History of Psychology. The "revisionist" influence is also strong in Claude Buxton, ed., *Points of View in the Modern History of Psychology* (Orlando, Fla.: Academic, 1985) and the recent textbooks: Thomas H. Leahey, *A History of Psychology: Main Currents in Psychological Thought*, 2d ed. (Englewood Cliffs, N.J.: Prentice-Hall, 1987); David J. Murray, *A History of Western Psychology* (Englewood Cliffs, N.J.: Prentice-Hall, 1983); L. S. Hearnshaw, *The Shaping of Modern Psychology: An Historical Introduction* (London: Routledge and Kegan Paul, 1987; New York: Methuen, 1987). The latter represents a British perspective.

Philosophical Psychology

Revisionist history and philosophy are interdependent, with many psychologists influencing both traditions. Revisionist philosophical psychology and philosophy of psychology are most evident among members of Division 24 of the American Psychological Association, Theoretical and Philosophical Psychology. The division publishes a semi-annual bulletin, *Theoretical and Philosophical Psychology,* which features articles by its members as well as relevant book reviews. Also relevant are the new journals, *New Ideas in Psychology: An International Journal of Innovative Theory in Psychology,* published by Pergamon Press, and *Philosophical Psychology,* published by the British Carfax Publishers. The following books are selected from among the many recently published volumes:

Barnaby B. Barratt, *Psychic Reality and Psychoanalytic Knowing* (Hillsdale, N.J.: Analytic, 1984). Influenced by the European hermeneutic tradition, Barratt asserts that the major influence of psychoanalysis is not the "return of the repressed" but an actual transformation of the self, leading to a transformed ontology.

S. C. Brown, ed., *Philosophy of Psychology* (United Kingdom: Macmillan, 1974; New York: Harper and Row, 1974). Proceedings of a conference sponsored by the Royal Institute of Philosophy in 1971. One of the first volumes featuring significant contributors to the new philosophy of psychology.

Kenneth Burke, *A Grammar of Motives* (New York: Prentice-Hall, 1945). An early work by a literary critic who explores implications of psychology for epistemology and personal ontology.

Allan R. Buss, ed., *Psychology in Social Context* (New York: Irvington, 1979). An early work applying the tradition begun by Peter L. Berger and Thomas Luckmann in *The Social Construction of Reality: A Treatise in the Sociology of Knowledge* (New York: Doubleday, 1966; Anchor Books, 1967).

Neil M. Cheshire, *The Nature of Psychodynamic Interpretation* (New York: John Wiley and Sons, 1975). With a thesis similar to Barratt's, Cheshire explores the process of transforming underlying mental structures.

Robert Cummins, *The Nature of Psychological Explanation* (Cambridge, Mass.: MIT Press, 1983). Cummins explores the difference between "subsumption under law" and "analysis," and explores the development of cognitive science.

Kenneth J. Gergen, *Toward Transformation in Social Knowledge* (New York: Springer-Verlag, 1982). In chapter 6, Evans criticizes this volume for its "relativism." However, Gergen's relativism applies to personal knowledge of the world and is descriptive of actual human functioning. It is not intended as a metaphysical treatise on the nature of reality. Gergen's ideas have generated considerable controversy and have established him as a significant spokesperson for the new philosophy of psychology.

Kenneth J. Gergen and Keith E. David, eds., *The Social Construction of the Person* (New York: Springer-Verlag, 1985). The authors examine how people come to describe, explain, or otherwise account for the world in which they live.

Amadeo Giorgi, *Psychology as Human Science: A Phenomenologically Based Approach* (New York: Harper and Row, 1970). An early work by a current leader in applications of the phenomenological method, reflecting the influence of Duquesne University's philosophical psychology program.

Rom Harré, *Personal Being: A Theory for Individual Psychology* (Cambridge, Mass.: Harvard University Press, 1984); Romano Harré and Paul F. Secord, *The Explanation of Social Behavior* (Oxford: Basil Blackwell, 1972). Following in the tradition of Peter Winch and Immanuel Kant, the authors examine the nature of action-meaningful behavior. Like Gergen's, their critique arises out of the deficiencies of contemporary social psychology.

M. H. van IJzendoorn and R. van der Veen (in collaboration with F. A. Googeens), translated by M. Schoen, *Main Currents of Critical Psychology: Vygotskij, Holzkamp, Riegel* (New York: Irvington, 1984). Emphasizes the difference between *Verstehen* and *Erklaren*, and explores ethical and political implications of this view.

Robert E. Lana, *The Foundations of Psychological Theory* (Hillsdale, N.J.: Lawrence Erlbaum, 1976). Explores the differences among predictive, theoretical, and phenomenological explanation, and the varying perspectives of subject and object.

Edward H. Madden, *Philosophical Problems of Psychology* (New York: Odyssey, 1962; reprint ed., Westport, Conn.: Greenwood, 1973, 1977). Madden's exploration emphasizes the problems of Gestalt psychology.

Joseph Margolis, Peter T. Manicas, Rom Harré, and Paul F. Secord, *Psychology: Designing the Discipline* (New York: Basil Blackwell, 1986). Follows in the tradition of earlier works by Secord and Harré.

Ian Mitroff and Ralph Kilmann, *Methodological Approaches to Social Science: Integrating Divergent Concepts and Theories* (San Francisco: Jossey-Bass, 1978). This text offers an excellent introduction to the variety of philosophies of social science, contrasting analytic, conceptual, conceptual-humanistic, and particular-humanistic approaches.

Jean Piaget, *Psychology and Epistemology*, translated by Arnold Rosin (New York: Grossman, 1971); *Logic and Psychology*, translated by W. Mays and F. Whitehead (New York: Basic, 1957); *Construction of Reality in the Child*, translated by Margaret Cook (New York: Basic, 1954). Here, Piaget explores the implications of his "genetic epistemology" for the philosophy of psychology. Piaget's position is explored in Beryl A. Geber, ed., *Piaget and Knowing: Studies in Ge-*

netic Epistemology (Boston: Routledge and Kegan Paul, 1977) and critiqued in Jean-Claude Brief, *Beyond Piaget: A Philosophical Psychology* (New York: Teachers College Press, 1983).

Robert D. Romanyshyn, *Psychological Life: From Science to Metaphor* (University of Texas Press, 1982). Romanyshyn is a leader in the current tradition emphasizing the role of metaphor and story in human understanding.

Joseph R. Royce and Leenderd P. Mos, eds., *Annals of Theoretical Psychology*, vols. 1 and 2 (New York: Plenum, 1984); K. P. Madsen and Leenderd P. Mos, eds., vol. 3 (1985); Leenderd P. Mos, ed., vol. 4 (1986). Papers in these volumes reflect traditions ranging from semantics (linguistics) to hermeneutics.

Merle B. Turner, *Philosophy and the Science of Behavior* (New York: Appleton-Century-Crofts, 1967). Part 2 was also published separately as *Psychology and the Philosophy of Science* in 1968. Both volumes were included in the Century Psychology Series, with the latter available in paperback.

Edwin R. Wallace IV, *Historiography and Causation in Psychoanalysis: An Essay on Psychoanalytic and Historical Epistemology* (Hillsdale, N.J.: Analytic, 1985). One of the most recent applications of hermeneutic principles to psychoanalysis.

Michael Wertheimer, *Fundamental Issues in Psychology* (New York: Holt, Rinehart and Winston, 1972). Wertheimer, who also wrote the popular *A Brief History of Psychology*, 3d ed. (New York: Holt, Rinehart and Winston, 1987), is one of the most articulate and readable of the current philosophical psychologists.

Gordon Westland, *Current Crises of Psychology* (London: Heinemann, 1978). Explores and attempts to resolve the crises of usefulness, the laboratory, statistics, science, philosophy, professionalism, publication, and ethics.

Chapter 1

Several excellent histories of the Thomistic influence are available:

Desiré Felicien Francois Joseph Mercier, *The Origins of Contemporary Psychology*, translated by W. H. Mitchell from the second French edition (New York: P. J. Kenedy and Sons, 1918). Cardinal Mercier offers a critique of Cartesianism and surveys the neo-Thomistic movement.

Robert Edward Brennan, *History of Psychology from the Standpoint of a Thomist* (New York: Macmillan, 1947). Brennan retells the history of psychology as a reaction to the philosophic tradition of Aristotle. A slightly different Catholic perspective is offered in Claude

Lawrence Vogel, ed., *Psychology and the Franciscan School: A Symposium of Essays* (Milwaukee: Bruce Publishing Company, 1932), which emphasizes the influence of Duns Scotus, and George Cajetan Reilly, *The Psychology of St. Albert the Great Compared with That of St. Thomas* (Washington, D.C.: Catholic University of America, 1934). A more focused analysis appears in William P. Witcutt's *Catholic Thought and Modern Psychology* (London: Burns, Oates and Washbourne, 1943).

Numerous examples of Christian psychology are documented in Hendrika Vande Kemp (in collaboration with H. Newton Malony), *Psychology and Theology in Western Thought 1683–1965: A Historical and Annotated Bibliography* (Millwood, N.Y.: Kraus International Publications, 1984).

Chapter 2

A cogent review of the various philosophical positions in contemporary psychology is found in Kenneth Hillner, *Psychology's Compositional Problem* (Amsterdam: North-Holland, 1987), volume 41 in the series Advances in Psychology. Hillner's particular bias leads him to reduce major differences to semantics, but this does not disqualify his concise model and the precision of his analysis.

The subtleties of the relationship between independent and dependent variables, stimulus and response, and cause and effect are explored by Joseph Rychlak in *A Philosophy of Science for Personality Theory* (Boston: Houghton Mifflin, 1968) and by James R. Averill in *Patterns of Psychological Thought: Readings in Historical and Contemporary Texts* (New York: Hemisphere, 1976).

The tendency of the human mind to self-deception is explored by David G. Myers, who offers a Christian perspective in *The Inflated Self: Human Illusion and the Biblical Call to Hope* (New York: Seabury, 1980), and by Daniel Goleman in *Vital Lies, Simple Truths: The Psychology of Self-Deception* (New York: Simon and Schuster, 1986).

Chapter 3

One approach to meaning which is relevant here is the symbolic interactionist tradition rooted in the sociological behaviorism of George Herbert Mead. An excellent overview of this tradition is provided by Joel M. Charon in *Symbolic Interactionism: An Introduction, an Interpretation, an Integration*, 2d ed. (Englewood Cliffs, N.J.: Prentice-Hall, 1985).

Discussions of meaning were vital to early introspectionist psychology, and culminated in Edward B. Titchener's "core-context theory of meaning." Titchener and his school of structuralists attempted to divest observations of "meaning," an effort ultimately doomed to failure. Discussions of intentionality were critical to the act psychologies arising out of the neo-Aristotelian work of Franz Brentano and culminating in the Würzburg school. These issues are discussed in depth in Boring's history, as well as D. B. Klein, *A History of Scientific Psychology: Its Origins and Philosophical Backgrounds* (New York: Basic, 1970). Nineteenth-century psychologists also devoted considerable energy to discussions of the differences between psychology and physics. These are also well-documented in Boring's history.

The role of the observer is addressed in the previously cited works of Gergen, Berger, and Luckmann, and the entire tradition focusing on the "social construction of reality." This tradition receives reinforcement from the work of comparative and cognitive psychologists, who have explored the significant interspecies differences in perceptual processes as well as human individual differences.

An excellent recent model for the study of emotion is offered by Joseph de Rivera in the following works: *Field-Theory in Human Science* (New York: Gardner, 1976); "A Structural Theory of the Emotions," *Psychological Issues,* Monograph 40 (New York: International Universities Press, 1977); *Conceptual Encounter: A Method for the Exploration of Human Experience* (Washington, D.C.: University Press of America, 1981).

The importance of intentionality has been repeatedly emphasized by Joseph Rychlak. Especially important is his *Discovering Free Will and Personal Responsibility* (New York: Oxford University Press, 1979), where he defines a *telosponse* as "the person's taking on (predicating, premising) of meaningful items (images, language terms, judgments etc.) relating to a referent acting as a purpose for the sake of which a behavior is intended" (p. 140). Another sensitive treatment of Aristotle's final causality occurs in Daniel N. Robinson, *An Intellectual History of Psychology* (New York: Macmillan, 1976).

Chapter 4

An interesting example of psychological hermeneutics is David Elkind's chapter on "Child Development Research" in the Koch and Leary volume (see chapter 1). Elkind examines the impact of an investigator's personal history on his or her theoretical work, exploring both the strengths and weaknesses which result for the developmental theories involved.

A much earlier example of the type of work conducted by Robert Bellah and his associates is Eduard Spranger's classic *Types of Men: The Psychology and Ethics of Personality*, translated from the fifth German edition by Paul J. W. Pigors (Halle: M. Niemeyer, 1928). This is rated by some as the most important example of *Geisteswissenschaft*, and strongly influenced the personality theory of Gordon W. Allport and the Allport-Vernon-Lindzey Study of Values. More extensive work of this sort was also done by the German group known as the Dorpat school: a group of religious psychologists following the research tradition of the Würzburg school. This work is nicely documented by David Wulff in "Experimental Introspection and Religious Experience: The Work of the Dorpat School of Religious Psychology," *Journal of the History of the Behavioral Sciences* 21 (1985): 131–50.

A number of historians and teachers of psychology are deeply aware of the insight-providing effects of literature. Some interesting examples are provided in the following articles:

C. Haffter. "The Changeling: History and Psychodynamics of Attitudes to Handicapped Children in European Folklore." *Journal of the History of the Behavioral Sciences* 4 (1968): 55–61.

L. Krasner. "The Psychology of Mystery." *American Psychologist* 38 (1983): 578–82.

J. Nyland. "Psychometric theory and the mystery novel." *American Psychologist* 39 (1984): 567.

R. L. Kellogg. "The Psychology of Agatha Christie." *Teaching of Psychology* 10, 1 (1983): 46–47.

Kerry G. Williams and Joseph Kolupke. "Psychology and Literature: An Interdisciplinary Approach to the Liberal Curriculum." *Teaching of Psychology* 13, 2 (1986): 59–61.

The importance of the moral philosophy tradition is recognized by most philosophically sensitive historians, and this tradition is well-documented in the histories by Fay and Roback.

A recent exploration of the contributions of Christian learning is Morton Kelsey's *Christianity as Psychology: The Healing Power of the Christian Message* (Minneapolis: Augsburg, 1986).

Early challenges to a psychology of needs were offered by Felix D. Duffey in *Psychiatry and Asceticism* (Saint Louis: Herder, 1950) and Johannes Lindworksy in *The Psychology of Asceticism*, translated by Emil Heiring (London: Edwards, 1936; Baltimore: Carroll, 1950).

A tradition which strongly counters the "selfism" of contemporary humanistic psychology is that of personalist philosophy and personality theory. Early personalists included such well-known psychologists as Mary W. Calkins, George Trumbull Ladd, James Ward, and James Bissett Pratt. This tradition impacted personality theory through Gordon W. Allport's *Personality: A Psychological Interpretation* (New York: Holt, 1937), a work which reflected the influence of William Louis Stern. Other integrative contributions from this tradition include Peter A. Bertocci, *Religion as Creative Insecurity* (New York: Association, 1958); Emmanuel Mounier, *The Character of Man*, translated by Cynthia Rowland (London: Rocklift, 1956); Igor A. Caruso, *Existential Psychology: From Analysis to Synthesis*, translated by Eva Krapf (New York: Herder and Herder, 1964); Paul E. Johnson, *Personality and Religion* (New York: Abingdon, 1957). The many works of Paul Tournier also reflect this tradition.

Chapter 5

One of the first twentieth-century psychologists to explore the relationship between facts and values was the Gestalt theorist Wolfgang Köhler, in *The Place of Value in a World of Fact* (1938; New York: New American Library, 1959).

Most of the revisionist historians and philosophical psychologists cited earlier would deny the possibility of a value-free science, and the assumption is no longer rampant in the profession of psychology. An additional source is Edmund V. Sullivan, *A Critical Psychology: Interpretation of the Personal World* (New York: Plenum, 1984). Sullivan addresses the impossibility of a value-free science, stresses the role of agency, and examines the role of linguistics and social action in the tradition of George Herbert Mead. An incisive epistemological analysis is provided by Gregory Bateson in *Steps Toward an Ecology of Mind* (New York: Chandler, 1972). A well-known recent work examining the value-laden nature of moral-development theory is Carol Gilligan, *In a Different Voice: Psychological Theory and Women's Development* (Cambridge, Mass.: Harvard University Press, 1982).

Also relevant to this discussion is the work on values in psychotherapy. Two excellent articles in this area are Allen E. Bergin, "Psychotherapy and Religious Values," *Journal of Consulting and Clinical Psychology* 48 (1980): 95–105, and Alan C. Tjeltveit, "The Ethics of Value-Conversion in Psychotherapy: Appropriate and Inappropriate Therapist Influence on Client Values," *Clinical Psychology Review* (1986): 515–37.

Choices in the realm of values and ethics may be related to stages of intellectual development or styles of intellectual functioning. An excellent statement of this position is offered by William Perry in *Forms of Ethical and Intellectual Development in the College Years: A Scheme* (New York: Holt, Rinehart and Winston, 1966). This model has led to research on religious development as well as the develop-

ment of an objective test designed to assess the stages. Such choices
may also be related to one's personality, especially when the latter is
regarded from the perspective of Jungian typology as described in
Carl G. Jung's *Psychological Types: or, the Psychology of Individua-
tion,* translated by H. Godwin Baynes (New York: Harcourt, Brace,
1923). Jung's "types" are most useful when regarded as varieties of
personal epistemology, and they parallel classical schools of epistemology and metaphysics—an issue discussed in Henri F. Ellenber-
ger's *The Discovery of the Unconscious: The History and Evolution of
Dynamic Psychiatry* (New York: Basic, 1970). This issue is also explored with great sensitivity in William P. Witcutt, *Blake, A Psychological Study* (London: Hollis and Carter, 1946).

Allport's *The Individual and His Religion* first appeared in 1950
(Macmillan) and brought a new respectability to the psychology of
religion. It was translated into Japanese (1953), Greek (1960), and
Danish (1966). Allport's work on prejudice, like that of many contem-
poraries, grew out of the troubling ethical problems of the holocaust.
His personal response to the holocaust is briefly but poignantly noted
in several of the "sermons" included in Gordon W. Allport, *Waiting
for the Lord: Thirty-three Meditations on God and Man,* edited by Peter A. Bertocci (New York: Macmillan, 1978).

Also relevant to the psychologist's choice of theories is Kuhn's notion of the paradigm (cited in chapter 1) and Leon Festinger's theory
of cognitive dissonance, as spelled out in *A Theory of Cognitive Dissonance* (New York: Row, Peterson, 1957) and reviewed by J. W. Brehm
and A. R. Cohen in *Explorations in Cognitive Dissonance* (New York:
Wiley, 1962). This theory dominated social psychology of the 1960s
and is reviewed in "The Principle of Consistency," in Roger Brown,
Social Psychology (New York: The Free Press, 1965), as well as most
standard social psychology textbooks.

The reader interested in self-deception is referred to the books by
Myers (chapter 2) and the Wallachs (chapter 6).

R. D. Laing's position is perhaps even clearer in the cogent essay,
"Mystification, Confusion, and Conflict" in Ivan Boszormenyi-Nagy
and James L. Framo, eds., *Intensive Family Therapy* (Harper and
Row, 1965). Laing views apparent craziness as the only possible response in certain well-defined interpersonal situations. Other perspectives on this phenomenon are offered by Jay Haley in *Strategies
of Psychotherapy* (New York: Grune and Stratton, 1963), especially
the chapter on "The Schizophrenic: His Methods and His Therapy,"
and Paul Watzlawick in *How Real Is Real? Confusion, Disinforma-
tion, Communication* (New York: Random House, 1976; Vintage Books,
1977).

Chapter 6

The secular psychological literature has produced several excellent critiques of the "culture of individualism." Two prominent ones are Alan S. Waterman, *The Psychology of Individualism* (New York: Praeger, 1984) and Michael A. Wallach and Lise Wallach, *Psychology's Sanction for Selfishness: The Error of Egoism in Theory and Therapy* (San Francisco: W. H. Freeman, 1983).

Joseph Rychlak's *Discovering Free Will and Personal Responsibility* (chapter 3) offers one of the best available summaries of the free will/determinism problem. An excellent discussion also occurs in Paul E. Meehl, Richard Klann, Alfred Schmieding, Kenneth H. Breimeier, and Sophie Schroeder-Slomann, *What, Then, Is Man? A Symposium of Theology, Psychology, and Psychiatry* (Saint Louis: Concordia, 1958). This study was commissioned by the Committee for Scholarly Research of the Lutheran Church, Missouri Synod. It is still one of the best available examples of integration. Psychologists must also deal with what Karl Popper termed, in *The Poverty of Historicism* (London: Routledge and Kegan Paul, 1957), the "Oedipus effect," the effect that a prediction may have to alter the future course of events. Also relevant are the discussions of Meehl and Radner in Michael Radner and Stephen Winokur, eds., *Analyses of Theories and Methods in Physics and Psychology* in volume 4 of the Minnesota Studies in the Philosophy of Science (Minneapolis: University of Minnesota Press, 1970).

Human choice is affected by a number of factors, including one social psychologists have explored under the rubric *decision freedom*. For further discussion related to these issues see Robert P. Abelson and Ariel Levi, "Decision Making and Decision Theory," in *The Handbook of Social Psychology, Vol. 1*, 3d ed., edited by Gardner Lindzey and Elliott Aranson (New York: Lawrence Erlbaum, 1985).

Chapter 7

Excellent documentation of the scholarly contributions of Catholic psychologists can be found in Henryk Misiak and Virginia M. Staudt [Sexton], *Catholics in Psychology: A Historical Survey* (New York: McGraw-Hill, 1954). Drs. Misiak and Sexton were both influential in the early work of the American Catholic Psychological Association (founded in 1948), which was the parent organization to Psychologists Interested in Religious Issues (since 1976 Division 36 of the American Psychological Association).

A theoretically ·and theologically sophisticated discussion of the relationship between belief/faith and psychological factors occurs in Paul W. Pruyser's *Between Belief and Unbelief* (New York: Harper and Row, 1974). Pruyser regards doubt as the antithesis of belief, and looks at belief and unbelief as positive and negative attitudes toward the object of belief. There is also an extensive social psychological literature on beliefs and attitudes and their emotional valence. Ongoing reviews of this literature may be found in various volumes in the *Annual Review of Psychology* (Palo Alto: Annual Reviews, Inc., 1950–).

In reference to the discussion on hermeneutics, the reader is again referred to Perry's work (chapter 5). Perry argues that the responses to relativism include not only nihilism and cynicism, but also an individually chosen commitment.

For the psychotherapist, the ambiguity of a text is nowhere more clear than in the art of dream interpretation. Jung's hermeneutical discussion in this regard, in *Dreams* (trans. R. F. C. Hull [Princeton: Princeton University Press, 1974]; vol. 20 in the collected works) is constructive, especially in its contrast with the more "certain" Freudian approach. In this same area, the variety of dream hermeneutics is nicely illustrated in Richard M. Jones, *The New Psychology of Dreaming* (New York: Grune and Stratton, 1970), which offers a variety of interpretations of the same dream.

Index

"Aboutness," 28, 48
Achievement, 84–86
Action(s), 68–69, 72–74, 79–80, 110–11; descriptions of, 89–91; freedom of, 121–28; meaning of, 27–40, 45–52; theories of, 76–77
Agency, 38, 69, 77, 118–19, 126, 128–29, 131
Agent causality, 118–19, 129–30
Aggression, 95, 99
Alcoholism, 41, 60–61
Allport, Gordon W., 97, 103
Anthropology, 71–72
Anxiety, 55–58
Aquinas, Thomas, 11, 76. *See also* Thomism
Aristotle, 76
Art, 95, 97, 99
Attitude(s), 52, 63, 75, 90–91, 136
Augustinians, 11–12, 14
Authorial intent, 139, 140
Authority, 95–96, 139–40
Averroes, 11
Averroists, 11–12
Avoidance-behavior, 57–58

Bausell, R. Barker, 63
Behaviorism, 19, 39, 46, 102, 111
Beliefs, 38, 90–91, 101–4, 126, 129, 136
Bellah, Robert, 17 n. 5, 73–74
Bias, 53
Biology, 43–44, 46, 83, 115
Body, 46–47, 137
Braybrooke, David, 25
Brown, Phil, 38 n. 11

Calvinism, 112
Causality, 38, 41–42, 58–61, 74–75, 112–16, 118–19, 121–24, 128–30
Character, 52, 54, 75, 109–10, 132
Chisholm, Roderick, 117n, 118n
Choice, 32, 57, 82, 112, 116–17, 120, 123–24, 128
Christ, 78, 80, 143
Christian learning, 71, 78–80
Christian psychology, 13, 16–17, 19–21, 40, 43–45, 107, 109–13, 127–29, 131–43
Church, 143
Clinical contexts, 105–6

Cognitivism, 39, 102, 111, 118
Commitment, 17–18, 113
Common grace, 129
Common ground, 134–35
Common sense, 24, 66
Community, 17, 20–21, 50, 69, 133,
    135–37, 143
Compatibilism, 114–18
Concept(s), 37, 51–52, 57, 62–63,
    64, 86, 94–100, 110
Concurrent validity, 63
Consistency, 12, 29–30, 121
Construct validity (and invalidity),
    62–63
Content validity, 63
Contradiction, 32, 105, 114
Conversion, 20, 25
Consciousness, 48–49, 84, 111
Correlation, 58–60, 63, 66
Covering law model of explanation,
    124–25, 127
Creation, 78–79, 93, 119, 131
Creativity, 97
Criteria, 15, 18, 24, 38, 63, 99, 101
Culture, 18–19, 30, 49–51, 72, 92,
    121, 138, 140

Danger, 55–56
Data, 14–15, 66, 100–101, 103–4
Death, 72–74
Decision, 32
Deconstructionism, 139
Deduction, 24
Definition, 54–58, 61–62, 96, 98–99,
    103, 110
Dependency, 61, 96
Derrida, Jacques, 139
Descartes, René, 76
Desire(s), 52, 115–18, 126
Despair, 83–86
Determinism, 21, 111–30
Devotion(s), 51, 53
Discovery, context of, 14
Discrimination, 96
Dogmatism, 94, 136
Donagan, Alan, 76n
Dustin, David, 55–57

Economics, 26
Edwards, Jonathan, 112
Elegance (as applied to theories), 15
Ellis, Albert, 37–39, 85
Emotion, 55–57, 111
Empiricism, 13–16, 18, 20, 23–27,
    35, 40–43, 54–55, 57–59, 60–61,
    64–70, 73–75, 98, 100, 121
Environment, 116–17, 120–21, 142
Epistemology, 93, 110, 127, 141
Epstein, Robert, 102
ESP, 101
Essence, 62
Ethics, 13, 31, 110, 133–34, 137
Evans, C. Stephen, 38 n. 10, 92n,
    136n
Event causality, 118–19
Evidence, 94, 100, 134
Evil, 77
Evolution, 117
Experience(s), 24, 49, 52–53, 70,
    110, 127, 140
Experiment, 35, 54, 59, 65, 68, 101–
    2
Explanation, 27, 32, 37–39, 42, 102,
    119, 122; 124–28
Extrinsic believer, 97

Facts, 13–14, 34–35, 88–90, 93–95,
    99–103
Faith, 11–12, 18, 51, 78, 97–98, 103,
    110, 112, 136, 140, 142–43
Falsificationism, 14–15
Family, 37, 41
Fear, 55–57
Feminism, 16, 38
Fertility, intellectual, 15, 101
Feyerabend, Paul K., 14
Fiske, Donald W., 62
Freedom, 20–21, 42, 57; and
    Christian psychology, 111–13,
    128–30; and determinism, 113–
    17; and hermeneutics, 127–28;
    misconceptions about, 120–27;
    nature of, 117–19
Freud, Sigmund, 39–40, 71, 83, 111
Friendship, 32–33, 95
Functional relationship, 58–59

Gadamer, Hans-Georg, 138
Gauld, Alan, 54 n
Generalizability, 54–55, 59, 65–66, 124–27
Gergen, Kenneth J., 128, 129 n
Gestalt psychology, 102
Gilligan, Carol, 38 n. 11
Glorification, 79
Goals, 61, 132
God, 78–80, 86, 91, 112, 119–20, 129, 131, 134, 137–38, 140, 142–43
Grace, 129
Guilt, 77

Hard determinism, 113–17
Hasker, William, 113 n, 115 n
Hell, 112
Hermeneutic, 34, 43, 50, 54, 61–63, 65–67, 72, 74, 127, 138–42
History, 71–72, 76, 119–21, 141–42
Hobbes, Thomas, 76
Holy Spirit, 80
Homosexuality, 102–3
Humanistic psychology, 83, 104, 107
Humanizer (of science or psychology), 20, 40
Hume, David, 76
Hypotheses, 14, 113

Identity, 85–86
Ideology, 41, 44, 135, 142
Imagination, 13, 51–52, 61, 69, 140
Incompatibilism, 114–17
Individualism, 17, 73, 88
Inductivism, 13
Infralapsarianism, 141
Instinct, 46, 83
Intention, 29, 49, 60, 77, 130, 139
Interdependence, 25, 40
Interpretation, 20, 25, 27–35, 40–42, 48–49, 68–69, 72, 100, 109–10, 134, 138–42
Intrinsic believer, 97
Introspection, 24, 48, 68–69
Intuition, 13–14, 24, 49, 92
Irrationality, 37–39, 126

James, William, 76
Jesus. *See* Christ
Justification, 30, 90, 95, 140; context of (in science), 14

Kant, Immanuel, 30–31
Kierkegaard, Søren, 52–53, 56–57, 83–86
Kingdom of God, 132, 142
Knowledge, 16, 24, 30, 35, 42, 51, 69–70, 87–88, 92–93, 101, 128, 135–40
Köhler, Wolfgang, 102
Kuhn, Thomas, 14, 17–18

Laing, R. D., 106
Language, 16
Law of nature, 15, 41, 112, 121, 124, 126–28
Learning, 102, 115
Lessnoff, David, 42 n, 125 n
Lewis, C. S., 90
Libertarianism: definition of, 118; view of causality, 118–19; misconceptions about, 120–27
Limiter of science, 92
Literature, 71, 74–75, 78
Locke, John, 76
Love, 72–73, 80, 84, 112
Luxury, 81–82

MacKay, Donald M., 115
Marriage, 38, 82–83
Marxism, 38, 133, 135
Maslow, Abraham, 24 n, 83
Materialism, 81–82
Meaning(s), 27–37, 41, 68–71; 73–74, 86–88, 104, 128–29, 131–32, 139–40; in empirical studies, 54–66; and human activity, 46–49; and observing behavior, 49–54
Metaphysic, 93, 110, 113, 118, 127
Method, 24, 64, 92, 103, 135, 139, 141
Methodological determinism, 113
Model(s), 27, 124–25
Morality, 31, 52–53, 77, 80, 82–83,

93–94, 96, 102–4, 112, 114, 116–
  17, 137
Motivation, 29, 31
Mythology, 114

Naturalism, 25, 90, 92, 107, 134
Natural science, 40, 110, 128
Need, 81–83
Network of theories. *See* Web of
  theories
Nihilism, 91, 93–94, 104, 107
Normative dimension of rules, 30,
  32, 36

Obedience, 79, 95–96, 99
Objectivity, 13–14, 24, 35, 40, 88,
  92, 106, 138–39
Obligation, 77, 80
Observation, 13, 24, 49–54, 88
Operant conditioning or learning,
  102, 134

Palmer, Richard, 138n
Paradigm, 117–20, 24–25
Participation, 50–51, 69, 75
Past, 120
Pathology, 57
Perception(s), 16, 52
Perkins, Richard, 25
Persecution, 135, 143
Person, 111, 118, 129, 137
Phenomenological psychology, 36,
  104
Philosophy, 14–17, 24, 73–78, 133,
  137–38, 141–43
Plantinga, Alvin, 11
Plato, 76
Pluralism, 133–34, 140, 142
Polanyi, Michael, 101
Policies, 29–30, 105
Political science, 71
Polkinghorne, Donald E., 128n
Positivism, 38, 76, 124
Possibilities, 47, 51, 69, 72–73, 116,
  143
Prayer, 51–52
Prediction, 27, 42, 63, 119–21, 125,
  128

Predictive validity, 63
Prejudice, 73, 97, 103
Pre-understanding, 72–73
Principles, 29–30, 107
Privatization of religion, 17
Probability, 14, 121–22
Protest, 34
Pseudoscience, 13
Purpose(s), 29, 77–78, 110

Racism, 95–96, 105
Rational-Emotive Therapy, 37
Rationality, 37–39, 56, 61, 88, 107,
  121, 126–27, 138
Rationalization(s), 61, 103, 106–7,
  128
Ratzsch, Del, 14n, 16n
Reason(s), 29, 103, 106–7, 124–28,
  141
Recollection, 68–69, 78–79
Redemption, 79
Reductionism, 53
Regularities, 26–27, 30–33, 40–43,
  104, 112, 120–21, 128
Reid, Thomas, 76, 118n
Relativism, 16, 107, 129, 139, 142
Relevance, 54, 63, 65–66, 99
Reliability, 55, 62
Religion, 53, 71, 97–99
Research, 54–55, 73, 113, 127;
  approaches to, 14, 18–20, 58–61;
  and regularities, 40–41; topics for,
  25–26, 94; validity and
  significance, 63–68; values and,
  101–3
Resistance, 13, 39
Responsibility, 20, 42, 111–12, 114,
  116–17, 128–29, 131
Revelation, 79–80, 92, 140
Ricouer, Paul, 43
Rogers, Carl, 24n, 85
Rule(s), 19, 29–39, 42, 50, 100, 104

Salvation, 141
Sartre, Jean-Paul, 120
Schizophrenia, 106
Science, 11–18, 91–94, 100–101,

119, 121–22, 124, 127, 135–38, 142

Scientific method, 13, 17, 135, 137, 139

Scriptures, 80, 134

Secular, 133–34, 142

Secularization, 93–94, 142

Segregation, 105

Self, 43, 84–86, 122

Self-deception, 43, 105–7

Self-esteem, 81, 83–86, 122

Self-interest, 37

Self-report, 68

Self-understanding, 72, 105–6

Sex, 82, 102

Sexism, 37

Shakespeare, William, 75, 79

Shotter, John, 54 n

Signification, 28, 48

Simplicity, 15, 101

Sin, 43, 57, 105, 112, 120, 137

Skill(s), 52, 68, 84–86

Skinner, B. F., 102, 134

Social role, 37

Sociology, 71–72, 95

Soft determinism, 113–17

Sovereignty of God, 112

Speculation, 66

Spirituality, 53–54, 82, 131

Statistics, 61–62, 66, 134

Story, 29, 34, 126–30

Subjectivity, 16, 35, 52, 66, 88, 91, 107

Supernatural activity (of God), 79

Survey research, 65, 68

Tacit knowledge, 101

Taylor, Charles, 28 n, 33 n. 9, 48 n

Taylor, Mark, 139 n

Technique, 61–62, 64, 66, 68, 70–71, 132, 138, 140–42

Technology, 58, 62

Temporal order, 59–60

Text, 28, 34, 48, 139–41

Theology, 19, 44, 74, 79–80, 110–12, 119, 133, 137–38

Theories, 13–16, 27, 34, 76, 94, 99–104, 110, 132

Therapy, 38–39, 70–71, 73

Third-party payments, 18

Thomism, 11–14

Titchener, Edward B., 69

Training, psychological, 46, 70–80

Truth, 13, 16, 35, 94, 100, 118, 129, 134–37, 141

Twofold truth, doctrine of, 11

Unconditional positive regard, 85

Underdetermination (of theory by fact), 15, 100–101

Understanding, 29, 42, 49, 51, 60–65, 69–75, 79, 128–29, 132, 134, 140

Universal thesis or agreement, 114, 118, 136–37

Validity, 54–55, 61–66

Value-critical psychology, 35–40, 42–43, 87–88, 104–5, 111, 121, 127

Value-free (value-neutral) psychology or science, 35–36, 40, 77, 87–107, 110

Value(s), 14–16, 20–21, 26–27, 35–40, 77, 87–107, 110–11, 129, 131–32

Van Inwagen, Peter, 117 n

Van Leeuwen, Mary Stewart, 23 n

Variables, 24, 59–60

Verifiability, 38, 124

Violence, 95

Volition(s), 115, 117–18

Walter, Tony, 81–83

Wants, 81–83

Web of theories, 15, 100

Winch, Peter, 29 n, 50 n

"Windsorizing," 15

Wisdom, 51–52, 68–71, 75–76, 78–81, 86, 110, 140

Wittgenstein, Ludwig, 33 n. 8

Work, 82

Worship, 30, 73

Wundt, Wilhelm, 69, 76